# Mugwumpishly Tendered

*Essays from the seasons of one woman's life*

## By M. Corinne Corley

Kansas City **WTF** Missouri

# Mugwumpishly Tendered

*Essays from the seasons of one woman's life*

## By M. Corinne Corley

Kansas City  Missouri

Write the Future
Kansas City, Missouri

Copyright © M. Corinne Corley 2022
First Edition 1 3 5 7 9 10 8 6 4 2
ISBN: 978-1-958182-16-1
LCCN: 2022943217

Editing:
Photography: Genevieve Casey © 2019-2022
Cover, interior design and layout: w.e. leathem

For Information Contact:

M. Corinne Corley
corinnecorley@themissourimugwump.com

Genevieve Casey
gcaseyphotos@gmail.com

Write the Future is an imprint of SPARTAN PRESS

Mugwumpishly Tendered:

*Being a year's worth of essays which originally appeared in various formats as part of The Saturday Musings, 2008 - 2017.*

By the Missouri Mugwump™:

M. Corinne Corley
the child formerly known as "Mary"

Photographs
by
Genevive Casey

## Dedication

Ms. Corley dedicates this work to:
Lucille Johanna Lyons Corley
10 September 1926 - 21 August 1985

and

Stephen Patrick Corley
25 December 1959 - 14 June 1997
*Fare Thee Well*


With Special Thanks to:
Joyce Elizabeth Corley

and

Patrick Charles Corley
for inspiration and strength at times
when I had neither of my own.

# CONTENTS

# Introduction: A Brief Word About Mugwumps

When I was about thirteen, my mother gave me a copy of *Emmy Lou: Her Book and Her Heart*, written in 1901 by George Madden Martin. The book follows Emily Louise Mac-Lauren from early school days to high school graduation. She lives with her aunts and an uncle but has an absent father who is a newspaper editor.

At one point in the progression of her story, Emmy Lou learns that her aunts and uncle are Democrats but her Papa is a Republican. She takes her confusion to her childhood friend Billy, who opines that she must be a Mugwump.

All of my life, I have felt that I did not belong anywhere. Like Emmy Lou, I seem to have one toe in each of several groups. I have never felt accepted anywhere but have valiantly tried to walk my road notwithstanding moments of intense loneliness.

In 2008, I found myself separated from my second husband and alone in my house with my son away on a student exchange program in Mexico. At the same time, several colleagues began a listserve for solo and small firm practitioners throughout the state of Missouri. This venue allowed me to communicate outside of my small circle of daily life and reach hundreds of colleagues who talked of their practices, lives, and viewpoints to virtual strangers.

Around Memorial Day that year, I posted First World War poetry to the listserve with some observations about patriotism and my conflicted opinions regarding loyalty to country. I signed that first email "Mugwumpishly tendered," partially in a nod to Emmy Lou and partially acknowledging the political use of the word, which described those who crossed party lines to support Grover Cleveland.

The tag line stuck. I continued to use it, and eventually started calling myself "the Missouri Mugwump," a name more poignant now that I live in northern California. I had always wanted a nickname; I suppose it's only fitting that I gave it to myself.

The emails that I wrote eventually morphed into my first blog, which I tendered weekly until December 2017. The passages in this volume come from that body of work. They bear the dates on which they first appeared. The photographs which accompany them are the work of a dear and extraordinarily talented friend, Genevieve Casey. Her pictures guide you from deepest winter to the mellowness of autumnal grace as you make your way through the seasons of my life by way of a year of musings.

Please enjoy.

Mugwumpishly tendered,


Corinne Corley
The Missouri Mugwump ™

# Saturday Musings, 01 January 2011

Good morning,

I hear the gentle sound of the little dog snoring. She sleeps in her tattered bed, head askew over the edge, oblivious to the passage of time and the turning of a new year. She knows only that her beloved boy has not made it home, and so she won't go into his room to sleep amidst the covers, without his long, lean body beside her.

My son received many admonishments to stay put last evening. The potential that he might consume alcohol and drive didn't worry as much as the potential that he might encounter someone else who had. His sleeping on a few feet of floor in a home where he spent many nights as a child seems more reasonable than venturing out into a city filled with amateurs attempting to navigate the city streets with impaired systems.

As for myself, I stayed home most of the night, after an early dinner at Charlie Hooper's, where the jukebox played a curious mix of old Grateful Dead and more modern rock, while the waitresses sashayed in time to the music. I don't have much use for the kind of tipsy reveling that characterizes the heralding of the new year. I am content.

I find myself thinking of all the times that I moved before I bought the Holmes House in 1993. I stop for a moment, raised coffee cup in hand, counting the places I've lived, and remember my first real apartment.

1

On Russell, east of Jefferson, the shotgun flat had two bedrooms and rent due each Sunday. My living room windows faced north, the view consisting of a long stretch of other four-family flats, brick, with their curved German-style windows. In the '70s, the street's occupants were middle-class working people, who left each morning early and came home each evening late, tired and dirty, wanting nothing more than a heavy meal and a cold beer. I did not know any fellow St. Louis U. students who lived that far east. I chose the apartment for its rent and spaciousness, for the clean if old kitchen, and the well-kept hardwood floors.

I had spent one-and-a-half semesters living in a hastily-found dorm room, after an unpleasant conversation with my mother in late October. I'm going to be late, probably won't be home for dinner, I had said. She barked at me in reply: If you are not home by 5pm, don't bother coming home at all. I took her at her word, to her ever-lasting chagrin. My work-study job in the Financial Aids office garnered me an increased grant that covered the cost of a dorm room until the end of second semester, and that first summer, 1974, I sublet the apartment of a friend at Russell and Grand. When she returned from home for the fall semester, I found a place on down the road, far from campus, far from the clusters of apartments in which my contemporaries lived.

That year, I dated a medical student named Ray. We usually met on campus and went out together from there, so he rarely visited my home. He would bring me back to wherever I had parked for class or work, and I made my own way home. I only have one memory of Ray ever being in my apartment, and that was after our relationship had ended, in the spring.

*You broke up with me because I'm black!* he shouted at me, in a raw, accusatory voice. *Ray, Ray, do you think it took me a year to notice??*

During the same time period, I had a friend, purely platonic, also black, named Hank. Hank, unlike Ray, freely came and went at my apartment. We fixed meals together, made fun of pop singers in loud, raucous conversations, and sat --- cozy, quiet, companionable, far into the night. Hank had strong, firm features; a short, sturdy body; and liquid, knowing brown eyes.

One Saturday, that spring, Hank rapped on the glass door to my apartment, hard and urgent. I lived on the second floor, and had to descend a long narrow stairway to admit visitors. He furiously knocked as I descended.

*Hold your horses!* I called to him.

I could see him through the window, glancing over his shoulder, worried, fearful. His polo shirt pulled tautly across his back and shoulder as he twisted around, and when he turned toward me, I caught a stab of the deep terror in his eyes. I opened the door.

*What's your problem?* I asked. He put out a hand to urge me back up into the flat, and I had just a few seconds to see what kind of demon might be following him. I saw only my landlady, who lived in the flat below me, standing in the yard with two rough, heavy men from across the street. As I watched, my landlady folded her arms across her wiry body, and gave her head, with its row upon row of tight pin curls, a jerk in my direction. I could not read her expression.

Hank continued past my living room into my kitchen and opened the metal door of a cabinet, taking down a silver aluminum glass. He filled it with cold water from the tap, and drank: long, deep, without pausing to breathe. He set the empty glass down on the counter. I stood a few feet from him, not speaking, watching him stare at something in the sink. Finally, he faced me. *I'm sorry,* he said. *I'm afraid I've caused you trouble.*

I shook my head, disbelieving that this gentle man could cause anyone trouble. He rushed past me and paced around the living room, agitated, insistent, telling me that the landlady and neighbors seemed upset by his presence.

*Sit down, here, sit down, calm down.* I touched his arm.

He jerked away and continued his pacing. I stood, helpless. *Don't be ridiculous,* I assured him. *What do they care who my friends are?*

But care they did. The next day, my landlady awakened me with a series of forceful, insistent bangs on my front door that reverberated through the apartment and penetrated the thick fog of sleep. I stumbled down in my flannel nightgown, long, wiry hair tumbling over one shoulder, spastic legs protesting at such strenuous work before the synapses had stirred. *What is it,* I grumbled. *Is the house on fire?*

She handed me an envelope.

*It's your notice, you gotta get out.* I stared at her, not awake enough to protest but aware of the ridiculousness of being evicted from an apartment with no more class than to cost fifty dollars a week.

*Why? I asked.*

*We can't have no coloreds here,* she snapped back at me, and turned on her tight little heel and walked over to her own stoop, disappearing into the door of her apartment.

I climbed the steps and sat in my living room. I looked at the shabby furniture that had come with the place -- a broken rocker, a bowed brown couch, a scuffed coffee table which appeared to have been used as a cobbler's bench and bore deep, scandalous scratches. Evicted. For having a black friend. And not even Ray, who had at least been my boyfriend.

I made my way into the galley kitchen, and put the percolator on the stove. As I waited for the first hot burst of coffee to appear in the little glass knob, I tried to get my mind around the landlady's comment. *We can't have no coloreds here.* In 1976. In a tacky little rundown neighborhood, east of Jefferson, in south St. Louis, where most of my Corley relatives wouldn't even want to be caught dead.

I spent the day gathering boxes for the move. I considered asking Hank to help, but thought that might just get him hurt. I had broken up with Ray by then, so I didn't have the muscle of a paramour on which to depend even if I would have asked, which I wouldn't have, for the same reason that I didn't ask Hank. I called a couple of my friends from North County instead, and started looking for somewhere to move.

One of those friends had a lawyer father. She mentioned my situation to him, and he suggested a complaint with the city. I pounced on this idea. The net result found a few hundred dollars in my pocket, which I used for a deposit on the next apartment, in Laclede Town, behind the University. My landlady admitted the reason she asked me to move. I don't think she even felt embarrassed. I'm not sure she knew why anyone would question her motivations. She didn't even have the decency to lie.

Hank had graduated, and left town shortly after my move. Though his full name has faded into the recesses of my old mind, I have not forgotten our friendship, or the hours we spent ruminating about the world, or that one, brief insight into what it must be like to face genuine hatred. I have not forgotten my glimpse of the fright in his eyes, or the electric feel of panic in his touch as he urged me back into the flat, as he pushed the door closed between us and that small, tight circle of angry neighbors on the sidewalk.

The dawning new year surrounds me, with its fresh, clean cold and the broad stretch of a pale sapphire sky. I shake away the memories and get up to pour myself another cup of coffee. I've several loads of laundry to do, and New Year's Resolutions to make. After a while, my son will come home, and I will hear all about the party he attended, on the last day of 2010.

Mugwumpishly tendered,


Corinne Corley

# Saturday Musings, 14 January 2012

Good morning,

The radio murmurs in the background, emitting the gentle cadences of the morning commentators who have peopled my world for many years. Their voices soothe me as I stumble around the kitchen, grumbling about the poor quality of my sleep, trying to keep my focus on the blessings in my life but momentarily distracted from that endeavor by self-pity. A man describes a hiking trip and the vibrant color of the woods through which he walks in the Adirondack Mountains. I stretch my neck and think about an upcoming Yoga class, hopeful for its positive impact. Another Saturday, another week, another seven days of tallying -- one for the "W" column, one for the "L" column or maybe just for the grey space in between. I never stop second-guessing my efforts -- as lawyer, mother, a friend. I never stop feeling that I fall short of a goal so painfully unattainable that my fingers ache as I stretch toward it and I only understand its virtue in the cold pit of my stomach.

I heard a story on the local public radio yesterday about a production at the Theatre for Young America. The subject of the play strikes close to home: bullying of disabled children. The idea of a hearing-impaired actress in a wheelchair playing a lead role so engaged me that I nearly struck a construction barrel and had to jerk my wheel hard to avoid collision.

I swear I experienced a flashback, to West Florissant Avenue, the long mile through Jennings, Missouri from the Catholic elementary school that I attended to the small bungalow in which I lived with my seven siblings and my parents. All those years ago, I huddled into my coat, book satchel thudding against my thin legs, and tried to ignore the gaggle of boys behind me. The trio staggered, arms swinging to and fro, guttural sounds emitting from their skinny necks. They called my name, and laughed, falling against each other as I quickened my tortured pace. I watched the houses as I passed, hoping for an adult to come out, see my tormentors and scold them.

Across the four-lane roadway, I saw the shamrocks on the shutters of the Clarke home and silently pleaded to Mrs. Clarke: *Come on, come out, and call me over! Come on,* I begged Marie and Carolyn, the daughters of the family, one my age and one that of my older sister. Born in Ireland, the Clarkes had clear and definite ideas about the proper behavior of children, and I felt certain that the conduct of the three boys who followed me would not rise to their strict expectations. But the door stayed closed; the house stood silent and forbidding. Keep walking, it told me. You'll have no safe harbor here.

I rounded the corner of my street, and the boys went by, hooting and dancing, thrilled with the impact that their behavior obviously had on me. I stood and watched them as they climbed the hill, beyond the corner gas station with the familiar figure of its attendant on a metal folding chair near the front door. He watched them, too, and then, with a quizzical glance in my direction, lit another cigarette. I turned away and trudged home.

The following Sunday, my mother and I walked home from church together. I felt the familiar lurch in my gut as my three torturers fell in step a half block behind us, oblivious to the potential of my mother's wrath. Their laughter drifted forwards. I quickened my pace, my legs jerking harder, protesting the strain of my speed. *Slow down,* my mother cautioned. *You'll fall.* No one had heard the word "disabled" in the early 1960's. My sister and I had a "walking problem," which the doctors claimed had "unknown origins of a genetic component". On that Sunday, I had no concern for labels, and only cared about whether my mother would realize that the children walking behind us created their entertainment by imitating me.

Three or four blocks into our walk home, my mother figured out what was happening. She stopped, turned, and stared at the boys. They stood still, wide-eyed and aghast. She took a step toward them, and they flung themselves in reverse and ran towards the church, their derisive laughter floating back towards us and settling on my miserable shoulders.

My mother looked at me. *Does that happen often?* she asked. I shrugged. She took my answer for confirmation and placed one hand on my face, cradling my cheek. *I'm so sorry,* she whispered. I knew she blamed herself. How could she not? She thought that she had failed to give me sturdy genes, and she knew that she had failed to give me a life that afforded me a chance to ride home in the sheltering confines of an automobile. *It's okay,* I insisted. *Don't worry about it. I don't mind those guys, they're stupid anyway.* I come from a long line of comforters. I spent my life lying to my mother. I never stopped. I never told her how I really felt, not once, not in all the 30 years we shared this earth. *It's no big deal,* I repeated.

She put her arm around me, and we started home again. After a few blocks, I realized that our physical proximity had caused her to limp in step with me, and I began to smile. I snuggled against her, poking her ribs, swaying my hips in time to her broken step, until she got the joke and began to giggle. We capsized against each other, chortling, holding on and howling. We slowly made our way down the street this way, sashaying, laughing, high-stepping, as the thin Sunday traffic slipped by, and the man at the gas station sat in his rickety chair and smoked his cigarettes, calmly gazing on us as though, perhaps, he understood.

The news has ended, and the Car Guys are now dispensing automotive wisdom. The morning rises around me, with its sharp clear air and its breathtaking freshness. With a long sigh, I glance at the clock, and think about the day ahead of me. The house sighs with me, and on the first floor, the old white cat curls on my son's abandoned pillow and settles down to sleep.

Mugwumpishly tendered,


Corinne Corley

# Saturday Musings, 15 January 2011

Good morning,

I have broken my fast with a plate of crumpets, yogurt and banana. My sorry little behind is dragging around the house, my body tainted by a smear of shingles rash, my face tingling with the nasty little sting of the bug. I have not taken the dose of anti-viral medication properly, and the episode lingers, even rallies, reminding me that better living through chemistry requires careful attention to directions.

My housemate tip-toes through the morning, then ventures out into his day with something suspiciously close to relief. I have not snarled, but neither have I spoken; and he must be forgiven his trepidation. I lift a cup of cold comfort, and gaze about my bedroom. I see the assortment of pens and other flotsam stuck into my brother's coffee mug, including a small luster-lace key fob that my son made for me a decade or so ago. This mug sits on the back shelf of my writing table with a few framed pictures of my siblings, a Haviland fruit cup filled with pretty rocks, and a framed studio shot of my son at aged 2.

Today is Martin Luther King's birthday -- the actual birthday, not the day chosen to give people a paid holiday from government work in ostensible honor of Dr. King. Several articles in our newspaper mention Dr. King; more on the Internet remind us of his life, his work and his message. As for myself, I have a curious view of relations between people who are dark-skinned and people who are light-skinned. I vacillate between my recognition of our country's history of bigotry, and my own unwavering conviction that we cannot accept each other until we stop dwelling on our differences.

I am reminded of one of the foster children whom my son and I sheltered, back in the mid-to-late 1990s when we served as a foster household. I can see this chubby little baby, Bianca; feel the warmth of her fat body against my thin frame. Her eyes glistened as they fixed on mine, as she reached and claimed a great gob of my thick, coarse hair. I see her in my son's cradle, at the foot of my parents' old bedstead, in the back bedroom of my Brookside bungalow. She fascinated my son, who was five at the time. He stood for hours over the cradle, or the bouncy seat staged on the dining room table, or the Grayco swing-o-matic in the living room. She clutched his small fingers with one hand while she waived her rattle with her other hand, and Patrick, in love, in love, in love, exclaimed to me, time after time: Can we keep her, Mom? Can we?

We could have. I wanted to keep her. I had wanted to keep little Kimmy before her, of whom I only recently dis-covered an endearing picture, at the bottom of a basket on a high shelf, saved but hidden, for fear my broken heart would not mend. Kinky corn rows sticking out from her delicate skull, inexpertly braided by her foster mother while her foster brother stood nearby; bright eyes; crooked smile. She spent several weeks with us before being placed with a "real" family, defined by her worker as one that looked more like her and had two parents.

Bianca came to us some months after Kimmy, but before the pair of brutally abused boys that would undo our resolve to continue fostering. Bianca had been born crack-positive but thrived, and by ten months, weighed more than Patrick had at twice the age. She demanded that I carry her every-where, around the house, through stores, in the park. I did not mind. With Patrick at my heels, I sailed around the house doing chores, Bianca on a skinny hip, chortling by my ear, grabbing at my glasses, happy.

Until the week that Patrick got strep throat, the situation could not have been more perfect. But the pediatrician admonished me to find another home for the foster baby until Patrick healed. I can't place her anywhere else, whined her case worker. So I did the next best thing: I asked a friend to keep her for a day or two. I called the case worker back, but she had left the office. I tapped my pencil against the table, thinking, before dialing the extension for the worker's supervisor. It's out-of-county, I explained. So I wanted to get permission. It is just for 72 hours. She approved it, and off went my little Bianca, until Patrick's condition allowed for her return.

The following Saturday, the friend who had given her safe harbor returned her to my house, with a few assorted children of her own. Patrick and I had struggled through the week, and my friend stayed for a few hours, cleaning my house for me, while I played with the baby.

I had expected a visit from Bianca's CASA worker, and she arrived before my friend and her children left. I didn't hear the knock at first, but Patrick did, and he opened the door before I could caution him to wait. I came up from behind him, holding our little Bianca.

The worker gazed first at Patrick, and then at me, with the baby in my arms. No one spoke for a minute or two, and then the worker said, in tones that still cause my blood to freeze, *You're white.*

I don't know what prompted her honest reaction to bubble out of her wicked little mouth. She herself sported fairly dark skin; I am 1/4 Lebanese but in complexion resemble my Irish father. Patrick looks like his father, who claims to be half-Scottish and half-Native American. But whatever little nugget of bigotry prompted her outburst, out it did burst, and if the room had been chilly before her arrival, its temperature dropped another several degrees upon her announcement.

Patrick tilted his head back, looking up the length of her, and corrected her assessment. Actually, we're beige, he said. She tore her eyes away from my face and fixed them on my son, pulling her brow into a dark, angry frown. *What did you say,* she demanded of him. He did not shy back. *I said we're beige; we are not white.* She jerked her head back, and spoke again. *And the baby's black,* she snapped. Patrick gently corrected her. *Actually, she's kind of Hershey-bar color,* he observed.

I pulled the door open wider, and motioned Patrick to stand back. I asked the woman if she wanted to come into the house, and come she did. Who are all these other kids, she asked. I explained. I told her about the strep throat, and the case worker with no solution to offer, and the help given by my out-of-county friend. I gave her the name of the supervisor who had approved the child's stay away from my home. I showed her the cradle at the end of my bed, and the toys in the basket, toys that my son had chosen for Bianca, from his own collection of beloved baby playthings. She barely spoke, showed little civility, and glanced, with disapproving skepticism, at the cobwebs in my corners, the small smear of jelly on my son's door frame, and the scuffed black cowboy boots that my son had taken to wearing everywhere, including to bed.

Bianca was removed from my home by order of a Family Court Commissioner on the following Monday. I protested. The ostensible reason was, of course, the child's brief sojourn in another county, of which CASA claimed they did not approve. My son and I cried; my friend offered to write a letter, which could jeopardize her own foster license in the county where she lived. The supervisor who had approved the respite arrangements apologized. The commissioner noted my protest, and assured me that he did not consider that I had done anything wrong.

The man who came for Bianca simpered his own regret in hollow tones, as he waited impatiently on our screened porch. I gently tendered her into his rough, rigid arms, and gave him the new diaper bag I had purchased for her, fully stocked; and a second bag, filled with small toys, books, and stuffed animals that Patrick had chosen. My son and I stood on the porch watching the fellow sashay down our walk, taking the child from us, a child whom we had planned to keep. *Bye, Bianca,* my son whispered, and a thousand angels cried.

I took Patrick down to the Plaza that afternoon. We had lunch at Winsteads, and then went to a store the name of which I can no longer recall, but which sold semi-precious gemstones in a hexagonal plexi-glass bin taller than my son. Patrick studied the rocks, selecting each one with determination, measuring by a standard that I could not fully grasp. When he had found the ones that pleased him, he carried them to the counter, and paid "with his own money." The man counted change into my boy's tight little fist, and solemnly presented him with a velveteen bag of the stones that Patrick had chosen. Later, at home, Patrick carefully divided his booty in half, and trickled one pile into my outstretched hand. *Those are for you, Mom,* he said. *To remember me by.*

My feet are cold, tucked behind my lily-white spastic legs, under the old kitchen chair at my desk. The house around me has grown very quiet. I am alone. Laundry waits to be sorted, and floors to be mopped. After a while, when my housemate tip-toes back from his tennis game, peering around the front door frame to gauge whether it is safe to enter, there will be lunch to fix. I will dutifully take my new course of anti-virals, and perhaps by Monday, I will feel human again.

Mugwumpishly tendered,


Corinne Corley

# Saturday Musings, 22 January 2011

Good morning,

The sun has climbed higher in the sky than I usually see as I write on Saturday mornings. I've slept a bit later; had coffee; eaten a Texas Ruby Red grapefruit, peeled; and read the *Kansas City Star*. I've traded idle pleasantries with my beloved, and kissed him goodbye as he headed for his 9:00 a.m. Board meeting. I washed and put away the breakfast dishes, and read a chapter of a pleasant novel by an Irish author whom I discovered at the public library yesterday. In short, I've done nothing at all, but the casual, first tasks of a day with few obligations other than laundry, and housework, and the running of errands.

I glance about the room, noting the chores to be done. I'm not an obsessive housekeeper. I make the beds; I put away the debris of weekly life; and I beat back the clutter that threatens to overtake my keeping shelf. Once a month, a college student comes for the heavy stuff, and every other week, I run a dust mop across the hardwood floors. Air filters hum between times, and the kitchen counters pine for a swipe at the end of the day.

I'm reflecting on mental illness today: the twist of thinking that drives a man to deep thoughts of self-harm; the jagged rush of chemicals that send a woman into hiding; the vile spread of gelatinous fear that overcomes a teenager just before she walks into a room filled with her chattering, sharp-eyed contemporaries. I have experienced sadness, and anger, and anxiousness; but I have been spared, I think, the kind of malaise that seeps into one's fiber or perhaps, exits within one's very genetic material.

Because I do not suffer genuine mental illness, I do not, truly, understand it.

Above the desk in my law office hangs a painting, intended to depict Venice. I can see it as I work; though more often, I am oblivious to it. The work has hung in every office that I have occupied since I received it from a client ten years or so ago.

Leah was her name. Intense, vibrant, driven; I see her sitting in my old office, an office from another decade, another century. I close my eyes; and her form solidifies. *They did this to me,* she urges. *Make them pay.* I gazed, without speaking, as she tried to explain. Then I glanced down at her intake form, where she had written the details of the matter that she wants me to handle. Military benefits.

I took in the gathering drops of sweat rising across the counters of her small face. I observed the tautness of her muscles. I listened as she talked, in rapid, jerky tones, about her time in service, and the young women who came to her, reporting sexual aggression by others. Leah had reported their allegations to her superiors. *And they locked me up, and they gave me drugs to keep me from talking, and they made me like this.*

The simplest analysis will serve this woman best, I told myself, gently placing her intake form on my desk. *You've got a diagnosis, and it says here, that your illness had nothing to do with your duties in the military.* Our eyes met. We both understood the portent of that determination. *I want to appeal,* she proclaimed. *I can pay. My aunt is helping me.* She stood, and I could not help myself -- I moved back, rolling my chair a bit further from her as she paced around the large area beside the small conference table at which we sat. She did not notice. *I can pay,* she repeated. I cautioned her, explained the potential futility of the appeal, the number of hours that I might have to bill, the likelihood of a disappointing outcome. *I don't care,* she repeated. *They did this to me. They did. I wasn't like this before.*

The diagnosis appeared multiple times in the small packet of records that she had brought. Paranoid schizophrenia. In the next box, the offending appellation: Non-service connected. No benefits. Medical discharge, back to civilian life, apply for SSI if you can, thanks for giving us four years of your life, we can't use you anymore. But Leah told a wild story of hospitalization, experimental drugs, retribution for defending the women who sought her help, the sexual harassment of whom she protested. If her story could be confirmed, perhaps the determination could be successfully challenged, and she could receive full benefits for a service-connected illness. Perhaps. Perhaps.

I pushed the little pile of papers to one side, and handed her a copy of my standard hourly contract, only briefly wondering if she could be said to be competent to enter into a binding agreement. She signed her name in bold, precise letters, and so, our odyssey began.

I started in the usual way: I filed the appeal, and then requested documents. Leah went back to her apartment, somewhere east of Main, on Linwood, in a tall building where the sick and the old lived in flats that used to be occupied by rich folks with heavy Victorian furniture. Weeks passed; and months; and paperwork dribbled into my files, small little packets of records of Leah's many hospitalizations while in service.

I shuffled the papers, idly, flicking my eyes through the boxes. Suicidal ideation, check. Paranoid thoughts, check. I ran my finger down a list of medications.

*Geez louise,* I thought. *This woman has taken drugs I've never heard of, and most of the ones that I have.*

17

I paced around my office, looking at the two-inch file. *There have to be more records than this,* I thought. She was in the hospital for six months, maybe more.

I sat down at my computer, and wrote another request for documents to the military attorney handling the defense against my client's claims. I read it several times, changing a word or two, revising my phrasing -- first more snippy, then less; settling on what I decided came across as mildly threatening but not indefensible. Save, print, sign, mail.

A month elapsed. Leah called almost daily at first. I assured her that I would let her know if I got anything more, if any progress had been made. I tried to bear in mind that her diagnosis suggested that she might not believe me, but if her paranoia extended to me, she did not show signs of it. Our conversations consisted of a brief query on her side, a disavowal of progress on mine, and her quiet thanks.

After the second week, she stopped calling. Time passed. We waited.

At the end of the third month, our UPS delivery person came into the office with a dolly full of boxes. Where do you want them, he asked. My secretary pulled me out to the reception area. I counted. Three boxes. I could accommodate those in my office, I suggested. He laughed, then shook his head. There's more.

We co-opted the floor's communal conference room. We arranged six tables in a square around its perimeter, and filled them with the cartons hauled upstairs by the UPS guy, in his brown uniform, his tall, wiry frame straining as he lifted them from his two-wheeler. *Who'd this person kill?* he asked. I chuckled. *Nobody, yet,* I assured him.

Fifteen boxes in all. Fifteen boxes, that I had waited more than ninety days to receive, and the contents of which I would now have to review. I called Leah. *Good,* she said, softly. She had not doubted that the records would come. She had more faith in my letter-writing ability than I did, it seemed.

18

A day or two later, I got a notice that our hearing date had been set -- in two weeks' time. *Two weeks? What's their hurry now,* I asked myself. I went across the hall to the cold room where my assistant sat, inventorying the contents of the boxes, and broke the news to him. *Can't be done,* he announced. *I can't inventory these documents in two weeks, and you can't read them in two weeks.*

We asked for a postponement on the basis of the delay in providing Leah's medical records. We got it.

The first snow fell. Thanksgiving came, and Christmas. Leah called the office over the Christmas holiday, leaving a message: *They've got me -- please help!* She left a number, which turned out to be the patient line at a hospital psychiatric unit.

I went to see her just before the new year. Her brown skin streaked with ashy grey, her tight curls awry, wearing a faded flannel robe, she pleaded with me to get her out. I just want to go home. I talked with the doctor on duty. *She's not a danger to herself, or to anyone else,* he admitted, *but we think she should stay.* My eyebrows shot up. *Why?* He shook his head. He was not the treating physician. He could not explain. My eyebrows went even higher. *I'll get a writ, if I need to,* I assured him. *You'll have to,* he said. Not his call.

I went a notch or two up the food chain, sitting in a dingy office, crammed away in the back corridor. The agitated administrator pushed piles of unread mail around on the scratched surface of his putty-colored steel desk, and snatched my client's chart from my hands. *The doctor thinks she should stay,* he grumbled. *But he can't make the standard,* I gently reminded, *and she wants to leave.* The doctor hovered in the background, arms tightly folded across his chest, wearing an expression that aroused my suspicion. Not concern -- not worry for his patient -- something else. Fear.

The two exchanged looks. I thought about the fact that no one knew where I was. Silence surrounded us, palpable, cloying. I did not relent. They did not speak.

After a few moments, during which more meaningful glances passed between the two of them, the doctor relented and signed a discharge order. I hurried out of the office, and found my client. *Get your stuff,* I told her. *Before whoever told them to put you here finds out you're leaving.* She changed into street clothes and we hastened to my car.

I parked on the silent, dirty city street where she lived. She fumbled with the damaged handle of the exterior door to her building, then led me past a small assemblage of residents sitting, wordless, in the lobby. Eyes averted, I stayed close to her, trying to ignore the smell of over-cooked coffee that permeated the hallway.

Leah's apartment surprised me. Simply, shabbily furnished, and small, nonetheless, light streamed in through large, clean windows and a floral scent clung to the fabric of the sofa and chair. But most surprising were the large canvasses everywhere: leaning against the walls, on wooden easels in the area that might otherwise be used for a dining table, in the hallway that must have led to a small bedroom.

I stopped, and stared. In vibrant colors, Leah had painted children of Africa. Not tragic, sympathetic poor children, but vibrant, alive, joyful little boys and girls -- with their mothers, with baskets of grain, with each other. In some pictures, she showed just the women, standing in small groups, seemingly engrossed in casual conversation, perhaps casting one disinterested eye over a shoulder at the watching artist. Her people of Africa did not beg for pennies, or bemoan their poverty. They simply lived, with no regard for anyone outside the happy circle of their existence.

On other easels, I saw a few darker works. A woman standing on a city street -- New York, perhaps, I told myself, from the sinister appearance of the alley behind her. Wide, staring eyes. Tense body. An absence of peace. The contrast between Western poverty and African richness could not be ignored in Leah's work. *Have you been there,* I asked her.

*Have you seen these villages that you're painting?* She shook her head. She gestured to a pile of magazines, from which, I presumed, she got some inspiration. Then she pointed to the picture of the woman on the streets of an American city, saying simply, *But I've been there.*

I left her, listening as she slid the brass chain into its slot. I walked more slowly down to the lobby than I had come up through it, and nodded, briefly, to the people sitting on plastic chairs. They did not return my greeting. I pulled my coat tight around me, and went home.

Over the next week, my assistant and I read the records. Entry after entry about Leah's illness -- its progression, its symptoms, its seriousness. We began to lose hope that we could prove anything of what she had told us. We found no mention of her having reported the other women's complaints of sexual impropriety by officers; we found no account of the experiments that she claimed had made her ill. We began to take a dimmer view of our attempts to have her mental state attributed to anything that happened to her while she was in service, which finding we would have to secure in order to get the benefits she wanted.

The new hearing date drew closer. I had spoken to Leah just a few times since her discharge from the hospital. She seemed to be doing well. She talked about taking classes at the local community college; she mentioned the possibility that her works might be shown. She asked if we had found anything. She did not get upset with my reply.

Then, just days before we were to have the hearing, as I read the last file, in the last box, I found what I had read through fifteen hundred reams of medical records to discover. One line, in one paragraph, on one page, of one month's reports: *This patient would not be likely to have experienced any of these symptoms but for the medications given to her during the initial hospitalization.* And the signature, legible, bold: A doctor in the branch of service in which my client had served.

I sat on hold while a clerk got the doctor's number for me. I sat on hold while a nurse looked for him. I sat on hold waiting for him to come to the phone, after he had been located. He spoke his name into the receiver. I identified myself, and explained the purpose of my call. A silence fell over the line. Finally, he said, calmly, *I've been waiting for your call.*

A few days later, I had official confirmation of what I had negotiated on the strength of the doctor's statements to me, which he put in writing. Full benefits. Permanent, full disability, service-connected. I called my client and let her know. She, too, met my words with silence; she, too, finally spoke in a gentle voice: *Thank you.*

Several months later, Leah called me. Her bill had been paid in full; her benefits had, presumably, had commenced. I had sent the fifteen boxes to storage, and restored the conference room to communal usability. Her case had receded into the history of my work as a solo practitioner -- one for the "W" column.

*I've got something for you,* Leah said. *And I've gotten something for your son, too.* I reflected, but only briefly. *Come to my house for coffee on Sunday,* I suggested. I had been to her house; it seemed only right that she should come to mine.

The doorbell summoned me that Sunday, promptly at the scheduled hour. Leah stood on my screen porch, with a large canvas covered in a sheet. She held a Tonka truck, still in its box but unwrapped. My son's eyes widened as she gave it to him. She pulled the canvas into the living room, and gently pulled the sheet down, revealing her painting of Venice.

On the back, she had written a simple sentence, thanking me for my work, and signing it, in red ink, with her full name.

The house has grown still. I've sat at this computer longer than I had planned. My legs have stiffened; my wrenched hip protests. The phone has rung but I have ignored it; I hope the caller did not take offense. I shake my head, and sniff the cup on my writing table, wrinkling my nose at the acrid smell of cold coffee. From downstairs, I hear the yowl of a cat urging me to come and turn on the water in the bathroom sink. I'll go and do her bidding, and then put on a kettle for tea. After a while, perhaps I'll start on the second chapter of my book.

Mugwumpishly tendered,


Corinne Corley

# Saturday Musings, 29 January 2011

Good morning,

I stretch my taut, aching muscles and shake the tingle from my right hand. Last night, I fell asleep after reading only 20 pages of a book on chronic pain management. I've decided that it is not so much that the pain is getting worse, as it is that I am getting crankier about living with it. I want to be one of those uncomplaining women whose epitaphs praise how much they bore without grumbling. I'm afraid it's too late for me in that regard, so I am now striving to be charmingly humorous in my constant whining about my fate.

I know I am fortunate. I've outlived all prognostications and at least one prognosticator. I've been publicly proclaimed too stubborn to die, too mean to live, and too irritable to be told which way to dance. But I have not done so with head held high, and stoic gaze, and dry eye. Rather, I have done so with sniveling spirit, and snapping voice, and more than a reasonable measure of stridency.

I am reminded, as I strain to lift my coffee cup, of one afternoon at St. Louis University, in the fall of 1973, my freshman year.

I struggled across the quad, against the beat of an early, cold wind. I pulled my camel-hair coat tighter around me, and bound the sash belt more snugly against my thin frame.

Shifting the pile of spiral notebooks and texts from one arm to the other, I stopped, briefly, trying to decide if I could cut another class. Look out, gang way, I heard, from behind, and stepped aside just quickly enough to avoid being side-swiped by a fast-moving wheelchair.

I watched as the chair, bearing a slender man whose fragile arms nonetheless worked the wheels with fury, zipped down the sidewalk and across Grand Blvd., and continued on, weaving around students meandering toward the buildings east of Grand. Amazing, I thought. I continued my slow trod to class, and thought no more of him.

Later, in the student union, I saw the man again, wending his way past dawdling young people into the pub. I watched as he touched an arm, nodded, and moved beyond the first few tables, pushing aside chairs blocking his path. He settled at a table in the far back, his arms drawn up, his head bobbing, the lean line of his jaw pointing towards the ceiling as his eyes pitched round.

He caught me staring. *You, girl, come on over here, get a better look!* he called. I closed my eyes in a futile attempt to escape the taunting cackle. *Come on, you know you want to! I'm a damn good lookin' fella, come on over and sit yourself down.* By the end of his second sentence, I knew that I had no choice; the entire noon-day population of the pub waited to see what I would do.

I sat down at his table. Someone brought a cold mug of beer with a giant straw for him, and glanced at me. *You want anything?* I shook my head. The waitress left without a second's hesitation.

He leaned forward, mouthing the straw, taking a long pull. *I've got CP,* he said. *What's your excuse?* I knew he didn't mean my excuse for limping. *I'm sorry,* I said, knowing the words were not enough. I looked away from his struggle to drink without meaningful use of his hands or arms. In my 18 years of living, I had yet to encounter many people with physical conditions more serious than mine. The Americans With

Disabilities Act had not yet pushed its way onto architectural planning; there were few "crippled people" as we used to be called, who could really navigate the world so freely as to be frequently out on their own. Only people such as myself, still ambulating though with difficulty, traversed the world on a regular basis until the advent of plentiful ramped curbs and accessible buildings.

He told me his name was David. I tendered my name. His interest drifted from the silence that ensued, and he saw other people, people he knew, and haled them. Soon, a cluster of laughing young men and women surrounded us, on chairs, crammed against the back wall, and standing. David had many more friends than I did, an easier demeanor, and a razor quick wit. He was popular.

I eased myself up from my chair after ten or fifteen minutes of sitting in the midst of their good-natured rowdiness. I put one finger out, and touched his shoulder. Nice to meet you, I told him, and he jerked his head in what might have been acknowledgment, or could have just been a random spasm. I left as quickly as I could, and the gap created by my absence closed around him. By some sad coincidence, a loud roar of laughter rose from his table just as I reached the door of the pub, and I could not help but believe that the joke was on me.

I saw him a lot after that. I learned that he intended to be a writer, a poet or a journalist, he had not decided which. He carried a tape recorder in a canvas bag hooked to the side of his wheelchair. He interviewed everybody he met, and went everywhere he could navigate on campus. People remembered him; folks in wheelchairs are not common enough to be unremarkable even now, and they were less so in the 70s.

I came upon David in the pub many days. He wore his straight hair long, and sported heavy flannel shirts over thermal t-shirts. *Coats are too much work,* he told me. I did not reply. I started sitting at his table, listening mostly, while he gently prodded stories from other students. I never knew if they understood themselves to be material for his work, or if they knew but did not care. *Everybody likes to talk,* he told me. He rolled his eyes to find mine, canting his head, manipulating the recalcitrant muscles of his neck. *Got that? Everybody likes to talk.*

He never asked me any questions though. My story did not interest him. I sat in a miserable huddle at his table day after day, and watched the ebb and flow of humanity seek him out. He would let one arm fall down and graze against each person as they sat beside him, but the arm would draw back up to his chest, tight and stubborn. His knees knocked against each other; he strapped his legs to the brackets of his footrest and kept them in a bound position all day He lowered his arms only to work the chair and get it going, and when he did so, great beads of sweat broke out across his forehead as he strained to force his arms to do his beckoning.

Towards Christmas break, I saw him with a girl, who pushed his chair, and stood behind him when they paused at lights. She wore an impossibly long scarf and had straight, waist-length hair of an indeterminate color. She had a tattered pea coat and tall, black boots with laces. She did not speak. *That's Susan,* he told me, gesturing with one crooked arm, one useless hand. She smiled at me with her mouth, under a slender nose and grim, honest, clear grey eyes.

I got involved in a play after Christmas, and got bitten by a brown recluse back stage during rehearsal one afternoon. I made the first performance -- *Look Homeward, Angel* -- and sat on the porch swing until the end of the second act, swooning with fever. My parents had come to see the show, and took me back to their house, where I sank into illness that lasted several weeks.

When I made it back to campus, I looked for David. But I did not see him. I would occasionally hear someone shout, *Look out, gang way!* and, turning, expect to see his small form in its metal ride, hurdling down the sidewalk. But it never was. His usual table had been pushed against the back wall of the pub, and the multitude of chairs previously grouped around it had been re-positioned. No one seemed to know why.

Towards spring, I stood, one afternoon, waiting to cross Grand, waiting for a walk signal. A small noise on my right distracted me, and I looked at the person standing there. I recognized the long, lazy sweep of mousy hair, and the arch of one brow over an unrestrained grey gaze. I asked her, *Have you seen David lately?* and Susan replied, just before stepping off the curb, *He died.*

I held back, unable to make my feet hit the pavement. I watched her cross, and disappear into the unending flow of students, living their lives, from dorm to lecture hall, from student union to the cool of the shady quadrangle. A horn honked, and I found myself standing in the crosswalk half-way over to the far side, crossing against the light. I stood very still, and waited, until the cars around me had passed, and then, lifting my tired feet a little higher, and holding my lily white spastic hands a little more easily, I made my way to class.

I focus, suddenly, on the quiet rush of the tinnitus with which I have lived for years, and the hum of the refrigerator. The sounds of the house shift around me, and outside, a passing car briefly revs its engine as it maneuvers around the two white SUVs parked in front. Lifting my coffee cup, I see that I have, without realizing, drunk another eight ounces of lukewarm artificial energy, and I think about making an egg before getting dressed, and getting on with my day.

Mugwumpishly tendered,


Corinne Corley

# Saturday Musings, 04 February 2012

Good morning,

I drag my sorry carcass from the heavy veil of drug-induced, fitful slumber, and struggle down to the first floor, where beans await my grinder and the dog scratches at the back door.

I spent yesterday afternoon at my in-laws' home. At one point in the pleasant afternoon, I looked across at my 81-year-old mother-in-law, smiling and nodding in her chair, half-asleep, hands tucked inside her sweater. I saw the tightness of her skin across her cheeks, and the frailness of her small forehead, with its thin sweep of white hair, and its porcelain pallor. And the years fell away.

I sat beside my mother in the last days and weeks of her life. She shrank to the form that I had not expected to see for three decades. Cancer prematurely aged her. She accepted her death-by-misdiagnosis with more grace than I could have imagined. She called me once, early in the eleven-month saga, and said, *An angel came to me in my dreams last night, and told me I have less than a year to live. And I'm all right with that.* I did not scream into the phone that she might be, but I was not. *I'm only 30!* I silently pleaded. *I don't have children yet! Who will be their grandmother if you die?*

Her angel had not lied. By late July of the following year, we knew. Weeks, maybe a month, maybe a bit more. We surrendered to the concept of her dying and started coping in different ways. One brother moved into the house to take the night shift, his nursing credentials an invaluable resume for helping in the last months of an ailing parent. A sister made daily stops at the house. Others came and went on the schedules that their lives allowed. Most of us drank too much.

I drove into St. Louis most weekends, sometimes confusing myself when I stopped for coffee then could not remember if I was coming -- or going. Is it Sunday? Then I'm on the way to Kansas City. Is it Friday? Then I'm St. Louis-bound. The waitress at the Bobber in Booneville became my ally. She gave me a free to-go cup of coffee and bade me to drive with caution, twice each weekend, for the whole long summer.

On the Sunday before my mother died, I sat beside her bed. I had liquefied her Dilaudid and leaned towards her mouth, stroking her neck the way we had been shown, to encourage weakened muscles to do the job that they wanted to abandon. *Swallow, Mama, swallow,* I coaxed, watching her forehead for signs of effort. *Swallow, Mama, please, swallow.*

Her sunken eyes bore a heavy cloud, and she stared over my shoulder at something that I could not see. My hand upon her neck trembled; the spoon that I held to her lips faltered. Tears slid down my cheeks.

And then, for less than a second, for longer than an eternity, my mother caught my gaze with her gentle brown eyes. The veil lifted, and she drew her brows together, and spoke.

*I am still your mother,* she snapped. *Don't patronize me.*

Startled, I replied, *Yes Ma'am,* a nano-second before the shroud fell back across her face.

It was the last thing I heard her say. She died on Wednesday, 21 August 1985.

The sun has risen, for what it's rise is worth in my cloud-encrusted town. In an hour, I will help lend a hand to a stranger in need, standing shoulder to shoulder with my friend Katrina and our families, as we help a victim of fire sort through her soot-covered belongings, desperate for something to salvage. So it is time to close the lid of my computer, and find warm clothes, and heavy shoes. It is time to tie up my hair in a heavy clip and put aside my memories. It is time to get on with living.

Mugwumpishly tendered,


Corinne Corley

# Saturday Musings, 05 February 2011

Good morning,

In the dim light of my upstairs bedroom, I feel a pleasant sense of isolation. The house has settled into a lazy kind of stupor. My fellow humans have left to fulfill their responsibilities out in the cold of February, and I have regressed to browsing through pictures of last night's opening of Penny Thieme's new show at the VALA gallery, clicking past pictures of myself in my current somewhat daffy guise. I linger on snapshots of a radiant Penny greeting friend after friend in a trio of rooms crowded with those who have always known that Penny's star would shine, the walls of which rooms bore brilliant witness to the fact that she has always done so.

Winter has asserted its own dazzling wildness into my daily existence. I bundle in down, and wool, and knee-high knits, burnished leather, and waterproof gloves. I sling my pocketbook cross-wise across my chest and lumber through drifts to my car. A stranger beckons with his arm and navigates me across an icy sidewalk. My neighbor scrapes my car's windows; my son sends an excited message: School is canceled! when Indiana feels the brunt of Nature's fury. It has grown impossibly cold.

I need but close my eyes to remember warmer days.

When I was in my teens, my mother decided we should camp as a family. She had fallen into what we called then -- and now, 26 years after her death -- her "hippy days." She cooked with whole wheat flour and brown rice. She stopped smoking, and took up sewing again, making her own wrap-around skirts in every fabric she found on sale. And she dragged us camping.

I am there, in an instant, feeling the heavy air of a warm day in early August. My father sits on a webbed lawn chair outside of a green four-person tent. I am thirteen or fourteen. My brothers, in one-pocket T-shirts and cut-off shorts, rummage around the clearing of the our little private peninsula, far from the RVs, showers, and port-a-potties. Beyond our encampment is Huzzah Creek, one of two tributaries of the Meramec River, south of St. Louis and an eternity away from whatever cares my mother leaves behind when she packs the battered pans, a dozen eggs, loaves of bread and cans of pork and beans in our old green cooler.

Prior to my mother's hippy days, my father's notion of camping had involved a cheap roadside motel and black-and-white television. But in the halcyon days of my middle youth, he gamely strove to please my mother, a kind of apology for the sins of the early decades of their marriage. Thus did he grudgingly assent to sleeping on a cot and missing a few days of televised Cardinals baseball. My brothers, on the other hand, thrilled in these rare and idyllic outings, breaking sticks for the campfire, gathering rocks, and plunging with abandon into the Creek. Occasionally, they ventured to the Meramec River itself, while I stayed in the gentler, more welcoming ripples beside our campsite.

On the last afternoon of our few vacation days, my brothers lured me upstream to the vigorous waters of the river. *Come on, Mare bear, you can swim! you can do it!*, they urged, stripping off their sweat pants and their T-shirts, preparing to swim in the still-damp trunks they perpetually wore beneath their clothes. I laughed, and sat down on a rock jutting into the water, casting aside my sandals and rolling up the cuffs of my blue jeans. *Not likely,* I replied. *Nice try, but no cigar.* I sat beside the river as they hurled themselves into its rushing depths, their wild laughter drifting back to me. I pulled my knees to my chest, and wrapped my arms around them, resting my head, letting my frizzy braids fall forward.

I drifted, half-asleep. The voices of my brothers receded, and my reveries shifted to the foreground. I didn't hear my oldest brother, Kevin, approach; and didn't see the grin he flashed to his confederate, Mark, on the other side. I startled, suddenly aware, just an instant before they pulled me into the water -- warned, perhaps, by the call of a bird in a nearby tree, or the deepest, most basic instinct of self-preservation.

I entered the river struggling, but at a place where even I could stand and hold my head above the water. *Come on, we'll help you,* Kevin told me, and each took a hand. With my bare feet sinking into the muck of the riverbed, I let them pull me forward. They guided me to the center, and then, with the current, we began to move in tandem. Just as slowly, they let go of my hands, and I found myself alone, moving downstream, feeling the encouraging kiss of the sun caressing my back while the cold, cleansing strength of the river pushed me forward.

With my eyes closed, now, in the chilly confines of my room, I lift my face and feel again the exhilaration of that day. I snap my braids, long shorn, through the air and lift my arms, sensing the warm wind rush over them. I salute the majestic, ancient trees that flank the river. I hear the raucous calls of my brothers, and other voices, other families, on the banks as I pass. With my eyes closed, I am once again the strong brave girl who turned, and, laughing into the wind, strode back against the river's pull, holding her head high, and her arms wide, smiling into the dazzling brilliance of an August afternoon.

Later, we scrambled to load our camping gear into the back of the car, and shuffled into damp shoes and clothes made grungy from the weekend's adventures. My brothers shoved each other, and Mother scolded them in an indolent, insincere voice. They settled against their respective windows, to my left and my right. I leaned against the back seat. As night settled around us, we journeyed home, and I fell asleep, dreaming of my walk in the water.

Mugwumpishly tendered,


Corinne Corley

# Saturday Musings, 18 February 2012

Good morning,

The pleasant murmurings of a radio commentator bare-ly ascend above the whirring of the furnace. Both remind me of the increasing weakness of my hearing. I move my chair closer to the one, fighting the intrusion of the other. The fat black cat purrs beside the register, casting a condescending look in my direction from time to time; in the bathroom, the old lady cat, my cancer survivor, yowls for me to turn on the spigot in the sink from which she drinks. Saturday morning, Brookside, business as usual.

The days assaulted me this week, long, heavy and oner-ous. I've come to the end of a ten-day stretch of unrelenting responsibility. From trial preparation to status conference ap-pearances to house-keeping and cooking, my February has yet to afford any cozy mornings or quiet afternoons. I should not complain: In my profession, being busy should trans-late to being financially stable, and in the pointed words of a judge for whom I prosecute, decades ago, *I woke up this morning, which puts me ahead of a lot of folks, so let's get this show started.*

Coming around a city corner several days ago, my eyes shrank from the force of the afternoon sun, which sat at just the right angle to blaze in my window. For a derisive moment,

I could not see the street over which I traversed, and I braked, full-strength, and sat behind the wheel for several long beats, transported back in time by a trick of my obsessive brain.

On 09 February 1982, I stepped from the curb on Wesport Road, halfway between Broadway and Pennsylvania in Kansas City, Missouri, into the path of a speeding VW Sirocco driven by a man from Persia who should have known the power of a setting sun on the sight of a Midwestern driver. His vehicle struck my left leg and threw me, by some uncanny trick of physics, straight up into the air. As my body rose, I told myself, *protect your head, woman,* and wrapped my arms around my bended knees, letting my head fall forward. Days later, a woman named Summer Shipp told me that she saw me fly past her office window on the second floor of what was then the Tivol theatre -- Summer Shipp herself fell to a murderer's wrath, not long ago. But that was half a life later, after she reached for her desk phone to call the police and report that a woman had just jumped from her roof, the way she perceived what she had seen.

I don't know how far I went above the street from which I had been catapulted. As I flew into the early evening sky, I rose higher than my corporal existence, and looked down upon my body. I saw the loose bun on the nape of my neck, falling out of its pins, sending spirals of auburn curls cascading over the brown suede coat into which I had huddled as I tried to cross Westport Road. I saw the little shoes pulled onto my feet, kitten heels, the only dress shoes I owned, bought at Bob Jones Shoes for the job interview which I had had that day. I saw my arms tightly wound around my legs and the sharp bend of my knees.

*I'm dead,* I told myself, as I lazily contemplated my small body rising above the earth. I felt myself suddenly suffused with warmth, and light, and a sultry sense of laziness that I had not previously experienced. I lost interest in the sight of my body and raised my eyes, searching for the source of the brightness with which I was surrounded. And I saw a startlingly bright being, hovering in the air beside me, with an expression on its face that I perceived as unearthly kindness.

The being raised an arm, and placed its hand on my head. A calmness spread throughout me, mild, and sweet. I bent my arms, reaching my hands towards the form in front of me, ignoring my body in its cramped little knot, still rising, beneath me. I heard a serene voice which seemed to come from the being that I faced: It's not time yet. And then the hand upon my head gently pushed downward, and I snapped back into my body, and found myself rapidly falling.

I smashed into the hood of the car that had hit me and flew into his windshield, bent knees first, and the glass and my right leg simultaneously shattered. The vehicle suddenly stopped, and my body, still with my arms wrapped around my bent legs, flew forward eighty-two feet from the front of the wrecked VW. I landed on the street with a sickening thud, and lay, still, unmoving, unaware of the dropped jaw of the neighborhood cop standing on the sidewalk to which I had been crossing, a hot coffee forgotten and sagging in his hand.

The world stopped turning, briefly. The unfortunate driver sat behind the wheel of his car, regretting his decision to leave Iran and come to America, to move to Kansas City, and drive a car on which he had no insurance. Summer Shipp froze at the window of her office, and the cop on his beat failed to notice that his coffee had drained from its paper cup. A small gaggle of nurses stopped on the threshold of a bar where they intended to spend happy hour. In the midst of it all, I lay, stunned, unmoving, thinking only, *Well, I guess I'm not going to die of a head injury, anyway.*

The wail of the approaching ambulance snapped the world from its stupor. Miss Shipp ran to the inner stairwell of her theatre and burst out onto the street. One of the nurses shrugged out of her coat and spread it over me. *Do you think we should get her out of the street,* a frantic voice asked, and I spoke, for the first time, startling those who were not convinced that I had survived. *Don't you people watch television! Never move someone who might have a neck injury!*

At the same time, I realized that my vision had blurred. I repeatedly passed my hand in front of my face, prompting someone to speculate that I might be hysterical. I think I lost a contact lens, I told the woman who by now had crouched down beside me, holding her body over mine, shielding me from the chilly winter air. And the paramedics descended from their rig, and my ethereal savior retreated, back to its heavenly perch, or wherever the Angel of Life spends its time when it is not immediately needed.

On 09 February 2012, thirty years after the car accident in which I shed not one drop of blood, I left the house and went to work. It was the first time since that day when I had not spent the anniversary huddled in my home, sheltered by one pretense or another. I made a conscious decision not to succumb to fear born of superstition. Ironically, my office building stands about two blocks from the scene of that accident, and I pass through the intersection several times a week, if not daily. But I've never gone to the scene of the event on the anniversary of its occurrence before this year, for the simple reason that I have never left the house on February 9th since that day.

This year, I had lunch in Westport and parked my car near the exact spot on which I had parked that day. I crossed the intersection just a few feet from where the car had struck me. I glanced at the second story window from which Summer Shipp had seen me, and thought about the terrible fate she met at the hands of a murderer who threw her body into a river where it was not found for several years. I looked at the restaurant that occupies the storefront to which I was intending to go that day. I thought about my bartender friend whom I had been planning to visit. I glanced to the east, at the intersection from which the car had turned, into the setting sun, which blinded him and kept him from realizing that just a few feet ahead, I was jaywalking without a thought in my brain that what I was doing might be dangerous.

Later that day, I went to my gentle yoga class. I stretched my artificial knee and turned the taut ankle of my somewhat atrophied right leg. I closed my eyes, and reached towards the ceiling with my extended palms, and turned my face upward. For a brief moment, I felt again the presence of that being, who suffused me with a light more wonderful than I could have imagined, and softly bade me to go on living.

Mugwumpishly tendered,


Corinne Corley

# Saturday Musings, 19 February 2011

Good morning,

The crisp blue of yesterday's sky yields to dull, mournful gray. As I made coffee this morning, I drew a sweater around my frame, then succumbed to temptation and kicked the furnace back into functionality. Its steady drone comforts me even before the warm air seeps into the room around me. I surrender to civilization. I am a creature of modern times.

As I crunch my cranberry-and-ginger cereal, with its organic claim to vitamin fortification, I muse over the morning news. I've dodged the union discussion so far -- pleading ignorance, demurring on account of overwork, shrugging off my heritage of civil disobedience born on an Austrian hillside when my great-grandfather shot off his own trigger finger to keep from serving in a war which seemed senseless to him. I read the LA Times article without judgment. I can see both sides.

The newspaper heralds approaching spring. As I browse its wrinkled pages, I think of other springs, other beginnings, other fresh starts and new arrivals. The contemplation amuses me.

I've been on the far side of a rising creek, a river's width away from my vehicle and consigned to an extra few days on a mountain top. I've crossed that river in a borrowed boat, astride a splintered wooden seat, with the mild threat of the rising water swirling in tantalizing waves around us. Decades later, in the city, as spring reluctantly moves into the vacuum created by the melting snow of a record-setting blizzard, I need only close my eyes to feel again the passing wind, the brief kiss of the falling rain, the sharp delicious rise of fear just before the boat clears the rocks and pulls safely to the dock on the other side.

My week filled beyond the breaking point with poignant faces. A man whose children fell into the system while he stood helplessly behind prison bars. Another whose former spouse moved their children to an undisclosed location while he served in Iraq. A woman with the faint stamp of drug addiction evident in a nervous fidget, who gazed at me with eyes of deep, fluid brown in which her hope of regaining custody had drowned. I shut the computer down at four o'clock on Friday, slid the last of the week's mail on top of a collection of personal belongings, and closed the suite door on stale air, dimmed lights, and tidied files.

I threw my pile of scarves, shoes, and jackets on the car seat and started the engine. On the way to the laboratory for my monthly tests, I dropped the letters in a mailbox, glancing briefly at two huddled figures sitting on a nearby church step. I saw their many layers of dirty clothing, and the crumbled brown bag that each clutched, and felt my eyelids flutter. *Look away,* I urged myself. *You've had enough.*

I parked in the handicapped space along the far side of the clinic wall. I passed a woman pushing a walker, intent on safely traversing the sidewalk and just barely clipping me with the edge of her over-sized handbag. Beneath the awning, a dejected, tousled man in green scrubs took long steady draws from a burning cigarette. I avoided his eyes and entered the building, taking the elevator to the first floor, and promptly getting lost in the underground maze of the complex.

With directions from a passing, friendly face, I found the lab in its new location. I entered, signed the log, and sat. Beside me, a woman texted on her cell phone, while her daughter meandered through a tattered picture book. The woman closed her phone, tucked it into her purse, and leaned towards the little girl. Together, they found the hidden objects on the book's pages, giggling, naming each one, chortling with each discovery.

After a few minutes, the woman turned to me and said, in a cheerful voice, *I like your shoes.* Surprised, I glanced down at my feet, instinctively tucked together at their customary, curious angle. *Thanks,* I replied, in a tone that seemed too skeptical. *They are made in Israel.* We both looked down, trying to figure out what that might mean. Neither of us spoke again.

But the child had noticed her interest and stood, suddenly, excitedly. *Those shoes look like dancing shoes!* she cried, and her little braids flew round her head, in a flutter of colorful plastic. *Are you a dancer?*

I shook my own head, but she did not believe me, and asked me if I would dance for her. *You dance,* her mother said. *Dance for the lady!* And the little girl shed her coat into her mother's arms, and in a cloud of pink and glitter, twirled around the waiting room, on her tippy toes, with a bright shine in her eyes and a wide smile on her earnest little face.

And my heart was made light.

The little girl's name was called by a technician. Her dance halted; she curtsied, and then, placing her small hand in her mother's larger, bejeweled one, she stilled her little feet in their sparkly sneakers, and solemnly went through the door, where she no doubt bravely submitted to the needle's sting.

Another patient exited, and I hastened towards the door to hold it as her companion navigated her out of the lab in her wheelchair. *Thank you,* she whispered, laying one thin finger on my arm. I nodded and sat. After a few minutes, I heard my own name, and seconds later, I sat in the technician's chair, waiting for the butterfly to penetrate the thin skin of my hand, as she chatted about her husband's latest tour of duty in Afghanistan.

And then, my week complete, I went home, feeling less discouraged, and perhaps, even somewhat hopeful. I navigated the streets of Kansas City with the warm recollection of that tiny dancer twirling around on the tile floor of the lab, with her shining eyes, and the world's most endearing smile.

Mugwumpishly tendered,


Corinne Corley

# Saturday Musings, 03 March 2012

Good morning,

Mixed news on a lovely Saturday morning: CVS apologizes for prescription errors that might have put children in jeopardy; tornadoes devastate towns in a long swathe that starts 100 miles south of my son's Indiana college town and moves down to Kentucky; a driver going the wrong way on an Interstate kills four, including three sorority sisters in one of three vehicles caravanning to the airport. Film at 11, ooh, such sorrow.

I write at the old desk in my second-floor room, blinds still closed against the early sunshine. I'm only half-attending to the noises of morning: my husband moving around as he prepares to leave, the dog snuffling in her bed downstairs, the chattering of the radio. I'm feeling a bit beaten; my body flags, pushed beyond its limit this week. Perhaps I should not have skipped my Gentle Yoga class; perhaps I did not consume sufficient quantities of water. Possibly, I am just growing old more rapidly than I care to acknowledge.

On balance, my week went well. But I confronted a first for my law practice: A client came to court in Elmo pajamas and fuzzy black slippers. Words truly failed me as I beheld her attire. She slumped her tall thin frame into the plastic chair beside me, and I struggled to think how to tell this nineteen-year-old mother of two that how she presented herself would materially affect the speed with which her children returned to her. I could see that she had no clue as to the folly of this last, small choice.

Later in the week, at a reception for the latest artist to share his works with my professional suite, I told this sad story and someone in the group asked where the children had been placed by the Court. *In their grandparents' care,* I assured her. She thought for a moment. *The maternal grandparents?* she asked. I said that *yes, the maternal grandparents had the children.* Another minute or two of silence. *The same ones who raised your client? Your client who doesn't know better than to come to court in pajamas? Those kids don't stand a chance.*

I had not thought of that. I had been so focused on the much greater good of the little ones not living on the streets with their mother, or in an apartment with her "boyfriend" of ten days. I realized, suddenly, that the grandparents might be, by far, the lesser of two evils, but it cannot be assumed that they are actually a good choice. The thought discouraged me.

The faces of all my appointed clients surrounded me in an insistent chorus as I tried to sleep last night. They were all there, loud, accusing, plaintive. I beheld each one in turn, become increasingly wakeful, increasingly tense, increasingly morose.

The mother of two who thought she was Hispanic because her children's fathers had been. *I think in Spanish!* she once insisted, from her blond, blue-eyed and earnest countenance. Her baby-daddies' families had sheltered her when she ran away at twelve, trying to escape abuse which followed her from her mother's house to the home of the aunt with whom the Kansas court had placed her. The undocumented workers cleaning the railroad tracks that passed over the viaduct beneath which she had taken refuge heard her quiet, muffled sobbing, and brought her to the abandoned houses in old Olathe where they themselves squatted. Ten years and two children later, a wild-eyed look testifying to unmedicated paranoia, she sat in my office and tried to explain how she had become Mexican, a process of reverse integration that I could not comprehend.

I drove another client to the rundown Craftsman bungalow on the east side in which she had once lived with her five children, and from which she would soon be evicted because she no longer qualified for Section 8 housing. On a frigid day in December, I could not let her take public transportation back from court, and broke my normal rule to avoid personal contact with appointed clients. The house looked as though it had potential. With a loving hand, and a little yard work; a paintbrush and a broom; the modest house on its poor but well-tended block might have been a charming place.

My client hesitated for longer than felt comfortable before opening the car door. I began to wonder if the address in front of which I had stopped was the correct one. She might not even live here, I mused. Maybe she already got kicked out, I told myself. But then she turned her broad, moon-shaped face towards me, and briefly looked directly into my eyes. *I just wanted to make a home, for once,* she said, with a long sigh. Then she got out, and quietly closed my door, and hauled her heavy frame up broken concrete steps, clutching the iron pipe hand-rail which swayed under the pressure of her weight. I drove away in the grey light of mid-winter, without looking backwards to see whether she made it even as far as the stoop.

Another day, another trial. A mother of two young girls, second and third grade as I recall. My client lived with a notorious drug-dealer and a late-night raid resulted in her arrest and later conviction. I had to writ her out from a federal correction facility for the trial which resulted in the termination of her parental rights. By then, the children had been living in another state for months, with a woman whose personal and professional list of accomplishments nearly qualified her to adopt my son, to say nothing of the two little daughters of a convicted meth addict. My client sat in clothes that I had procured for her, into which she changed after the guard reluctantly removed her shackles, in a small room behind the commissioner's chambers. Tears streamed down her face through the entire proceeding, including the fifteen painful moments when she sat in the witness box and tried to explain herself, against my advice, against all reason.

In my large corner office, with its oak table, the picture of my grandfather, and the framed Lafayette Square posters that I salvaged from the debris of my brother's life, I stood last evening talking to a couple of first-year law students. Impossibly young, with light, bright eyes and smooth, eager faces, these 1Ls exclaimed at the nontraditional furnishings surrounding them. *This doesn't look like a lawyer's office,* they cried, with a tone that told me that they could not quite believe what they saw. I'm not sure if "not looking like a lawyer's office" seemed desirable to them, but I thanked them, and turned the conversation down safer avenues.

Later, straightening our lovely suite after the artist's reception we held last evening, I reflected on the concept of not looking like a lawyer's office, and by extrapolation, not looking like a lawyer. That description has never more aptly applied to me. I own only one suit, which I bought second-hand for seven dollars. I catch my unruly Lebanese curls in a big plastic clip on the back of my head, and only under duress. I don't charge by the hour and I never bill for time spent talking to my client on the phone or even for meeting with them face-to-face. I'll never be rich. I never turn down Juvenile court appointments.

And I am still haunted by each and every one of them, when I lie in bed at night, blind without my glasses, clearly seeing, nonetheless, the eternal pleading on the faces of the unrestful ghosts which crowd around me.

Mugwumpishly tendered,


Corinne Corley

# Saturday Musings, 05 March 2011

Good morning,

I raise the blind above my desk and gaze out of a dirt-streaked window at the soft sky, with its thin trails of white wistful clouds. Against this delicate backdrop, bare trees rise stark and black. Perhaps small buds of new leaves pepper the branches, but I cannot see them from this distance, and the sky looks to be clutched in winter's wicked grasp.

Nearly one-third of this year has dribbled through my fingers as I reached to grasp it. I am astonished at how quickly the time passes. I convince myself that the rate of minutes accelerates, though surely it does not. Surely, my obligations merely expand to clutter the days and send me careening from dawn to dusk, collapsing in exhaustion for a few meager hours before I rise and race against the staring clock with its rushing hands.

I don't know when my life became this frantic. But I suspect I share a common malady with many. I listened to an NPR story about a company developing plastic that doesn't poison us, and wondered how we ever came to use receptacles that do pose such threat. Surely, glass can hold milk without contaminating it. We strove to make our lives disposable for decade upon decade, only to learn that the means for such convenience now clog our sewers, kill our wildlife, and sicken our children.

From where I sit, I can see a "dish," with its metal protrusion gesturing in a manner only vaguely obscene. I suppose it catches some sort of signal that its minders claim does not damage anything else through which it passes. I begin to understand the craze-eyed wanderers with their tin foil helmets. The world sinks into strangeness, and I stand, observing, wondering what conveniences do not carry health risks, or make us lazy, or deafen our ears.

I remember simpler times. And I wonder, as I remember them, if they were better than the times in which we now live.

I used to say that my family "was poor," until I met genuine poverty, and now I simply say, "we were middle class." We sometimes lacked for sufficient food, though we never starved. A broken jug of milk evoked tears; and my clothes lagged a season or two behind those of my parochial classmates. But we did not wander the streets for lack of a bed or a roof, and grandparents helped if the money ran short.

Still, our play grew creative because our playthings fell into the rudimentary category. Perhaps we had what others had in those days, before video games and iPods. Perhaps we had less. Either way, the toys of my youth had no motors, and much of my childhood occurred out-of-doors. This was especially true in the summer, when we had free license to wander from after breakfast until the street lights came on in our neighborhood.

Down the street from my house, the railroad track passed a small commercial outfit. As I reflect back to those days, I can't recall the nature of that business. It could have had something to do with rail shipping; perhaps maintenance crews for the railway stored their tools in the locked shed. I can't say. But we played there, I'm sure against the instructions of our working mother. We scrapped among the rocks by the side of the railroad tracks, and used the corrugated tin buildings as targets.

A block up from that juncture, a business lay empty, or so it appeared to me. Its grounds mostly held a large pool of something dank and smelly. I don't recall that business ever being active but I do vaguely recall that at one time, it made X-ray developer. I'm not sure what purpose the pool served.

One day, I wandered as far as the old factory without any of my siblings. I pushed aside the rusty gate, opening it far enough to slip into the yard. I felt my way among the broken bricks, and stood above the stinking liquid of the large cesspool. My eyes glazed as I stared into its depths. I breathed the stench of the chemicals, and felt my head swoon. As the world darkened around me, I began to pitch, head first, into the well of filth below me.

A large, dark hand pulled me back and threw me down upon the cinder driveway. I stared at the face hovering over me, with its deep lines and heavy fringe of graying hair. Denim surrounded the unshaven, wrinkled neck, a jacket streaked with oil and grime. I pulled myself up, and the man stood back away from me. Neither of us spoke. My head cleared, and I inched away. When I had cleared the gap in the gate, I began to run, three blocks to my house and on down the driveway, then through our backdoor.

I threw myself into a chair in the breakfast room. I felt the sweat rise on my face and dribble down the back of my neck. My braids hung dank and clammy against my chest; my shirt stuck to my skin. The fumes that had risen from the factory's pool clung to my clothing. I shed it quickly, and stepped into a hot shower.

By the time my brothers came home from their afternoon bike ride, I had found a book, and thrown myself into the adventures within its pages. I did not tell them what had happened. I never wandered to that place again, and I never saw the man who saved me. I never thanked him.

A bird squawks outside my window, reminding me that the morning wanes. Downstairs, the black cat yowls to be released into the wild. I rise to oblige him, thinking that perhaps, the world is safe enough for my tom cat.

Mugwumpishly tendered,


Corinne Corley

# Saturday Musings, 12 March 2011

Good morning,

Last evening, I heard a singer whose voice had a lilting, Spanish accent stealing the attention of diners at a Mexican restaurant in Waldo. My first listen caused my brow to wrinkle. But when he switched from American pop covers to the cadences of his birth land, his voice mellowed, and the diners set down their forks to genuinely listen.

I am continually struck by the differences that make our world sometimes joyful, sometimes disturbing. Conservative, liberal, Catholic, Muslim, Jewish, brown, beige, pale: we strut around pushing our small rocks of weight against each other's space and demanding attention. I sit and listen to the rousing, rough debate -- in Wisconsin, in Washington, around the nation and the world. I hear the words "stalemate," "reckless," and "unconstitutional" intermingled with the words "freedom," "stability," and "liberty." I wonder if it matters. I worry that it is all given more importance than it deserves, and that the drive to win improperly colors the judgment of those who compete.

In a nearly empty courtroom this week, I watched a small, fretful woman twitch and toss a head of unnaturally blond, pressed hair. She glared at the man on the stand whom I represented, bursting out occasionally in protest at his accusations. When she took the stand, she admitted her drug use in ferocious, swaggering tones while begging for her son to remain in her home. She must have known -- as my client knew, and I knew, and the judge knew, that her addiction precluded such result. No one condemned her. Everyone pitied her. She slunk down from the witness stand and trudged the few feet to her chair, crumpling into it and sinking back into her leather jacket, pulling its collar over her face. No one spoke except the judge, who closed the proceedings with a few gentle comments, taking it under advisement, though his ruling came within a day. *Motion for change of residential custody, granted.* I felt it as a shallow victory, though perhaps a child had been saved from the folly that might otherwise have awaited him, in the clutches of an addict who thinks nothing of taking him with her on drug buys.

When I returned from court that day, I texted my own son, wondering which of my choices exposed him to potential harm. I pulled several files toward me, and, with the push of an inexplicable drive, I worked each one. With untiring ferocity, I sent paper into the outer limits of the Internet for review by clients. I tendered letters into the morass of the postal service, left voice-mail messages, and reviewed reams of paper sent by other lawyers from other desks, in other offices, driven by other unseen forces. By the end of the day, I had touched each of my cases, pushing the boulder just a little farther up the hill, propping it with a strong lever.

Yesterday, I heard a story on NPR about a recently written book detailing the events of the attempted assassination of President Reagan. I listened to the author describe the actions of the operating room personnel, and to the Secret Service agent who saved the President's life quietly tell why he decided to change the course of our history by diverting the limousine to the hospital despite Mr. Reagan's mumbled assurances that he did not need medical attention.

I reached my destination as the story ended. Sitting in my car, I closed my eyes and recalled, as I had not remembered for years, the split second when I reached for a seat belt just before a car slammed into the door of the vehicle in which I rode. Because I had not yet restrained myself, the powerful impact turned my body sideways, and my hip bore the crush of the other car's wheel instead of my pelvis.

I thought about the force of another car, a decade later, that sent me flying high enough to be seen by a woman in her second floor office, who called 911 as I sailed back down and slammed onto the hood of the car that hit me. The woman in that office visited me in the hospital, just to be sure I had survived. Years later, Summer Shipp died a savage, lonely death at the hands of a man bent on committing a vicious, senseless act. Her body settled in the bed of a river, and there it rested for a long time, while her family and all of Kansas City searched for her, hoping to discover that she had simply gotten lost, or suffered amnesia, or merely absconded.

The world turns. In a split second, its cracks shift and a country reels. Its oceans rise and slam into the acres of cement and steel that we have constructed. A body slumps. A child dies. On the table in my dining room, the shell of an amaryllis bulb thrusts out a shoot long after I had decided its life must have ended. In another few days, a bloom will appear, bright pink on a vivid green stalk. As I eat my breakfast, I gaze upon the sturdy frond rising above the pebbles in the crock, and I dare to think that somewhere, in a neighborhood not too far from my home, a twelve-year old boy secretly sighs in sweet relief, to be waking in a home with a sober parent.

Mugwumpishly tendered,


Corinne Corley

# Saturday Musings, 31 March 2012

Good morning,

The distant sound of a train echoes around me. My wakefulness draws me to the computer's keyboard. With a press of the mute button, I mask the ticking of my letters, so that nothing I do lends itself to the otherwise still aura of the bedroom. Night time, Brookside, another sleepless night.

I feel a tantalizing chill through the open window which carries the gentle fragrance of an early spring. The height of the room captures the breeze coming off the neighbor's trees, triggering a mild lament at the deliberate loss of our old cedar and the bold mimosa which I had cultivated from a volunteer sapling. In their place, a clump of holly barely clears the height of a dainty woman. No breeze stirs this shrub. But behind our house, beyond the ugly fencing that my neighbor installed, tall, old limbs toss the night air in my direction.

I recall an autumn night in Montana, when I descended from Glacier Park in the stillness of All Hallows Eve, past rows of white crosses marking tragic losses on the highway, past skittering, costumed children running from house to house on the deliciously eerie streets in a series of minuscule towns. I think of a summer evening on a stone porch in Boulder, my young son seated on the bench beside me, playing with trucks as I half-listened to the murmurs of a heated conversation inside the house. The argument had nothing to do with us. We had come along on a road trip to take my son's friend for summer visitation with his father. Those in the house fretted about the logistics of the exchange: the length of the visit; whether we should return at the visit's end or let the boy come home, alone, by plane, by bus, by train. They argued amongst themselves before delivering the child to his father the next morning; it was all war strategy, I thought, idly, lifting my face to the warmth of the summer night. Futile, destined to failure, a distraction from the grace of the mountains around us.

Rummaging through my cedar closet a few days ago, I found an envelope of pictures taken at a mountain festival, held in Arkansas, in the rolling hills above Jasper. I ran my finger along the shiny photo paper, over the faces of people whose names I can no longer remember. Sorting through the small stack of photographs, I shivered, feeling again the prickling of the summer sun, the rise of a light burn on my skin. In one photo, a wiry, slender woman's long black braid falls forward over her shoulder as she hoists folding chairs from the back of a pick-up. Nearby, a man stands on the middle rung of a ladder, glancing over his shoulder, crinkling his leathery skin in a deep, uncensored smile just as the shutter clicks. I can still feel the soft crunch of dirt under my feet, still hear the dancing tune of a fiddle, the call of children on the hill above the community center. I can almost taste the tender corn, roasted in its husk inside an old metal drum, basted in peanut butter that oozed out of the foil wrapping and ran down my fingers. I can smell the pungent fragrance of home grown tomatoes sprinkled with fresh, tender basil.

On a mild evening this week, I drove home from work through the Plaza. The slow traffic near Brush Creek irked me. As I waited for a traffic light to change in my favor, I glanced out of the open passenger window and saw a woman walking behind a small girl. The little one bent forward, golden curls sweetly arranged around her thin, pale face. She wore a light spring coat over a ruffled skirt that clung to her knobby knees. Her frail arms strained, each tiny hand gripping the frame of a wheeled walker, which she pushed forward as she took halting, painful steps. I could not see the woman's face. But I could see the child clearly. I judged her to be about four. The light changed, and I drove slowly by the two. The mother kept a few paces behind her child, watching but not interfering. I noticed the glint of metal braces encasing the child's legs. I tried to find her in my rear view mirror as I made my way over the bridge, but the traffic surged, blocking my view. I continued on, subdued, my irritation slipping away.

Outside my house, the train has long since continued on its journey and the night has fallen quiet. March did not come in like a roaring feline, and it is exiting, this March of 2012, like a languid river carrying a gliding longboat on an unhurried journey. April Fool's Day beckons; Easter rides its heels. I close my eyes, leaning toward the open window. If I hold myself impossibly still, taking long, deliberate breaths, I can capture the scent of lilacs, washing over me, on an early spring night, in Brookside, in Kansas City, as I wait for sleep to offer its elusive embrace.

Mugwumpishly tendered,


Corinne Corley

# Monday Morning Musings, 09 April 2012

Good morning, and a good morning it is.

I've a story to tell, and it is mostly a borrowed story. So indulge me. Picture this story told by a woman to her children. The woman is about 5 feet three, early to mid 50s, greying auburn hair, short, sassy, always a quick smile but sometimes a tense frown adorning her face.

Oh wait. That could be me.

So thought I, on Friday afternoon, lying in a hospital bed in St. Luke's brand-spanking new Heart Institute, listening to the overly condescending voice of the admitting nurse and thinking of a story that my mother once shared, about using the same tone with someone in the hospital at which she worked. The circle, indeed, is unbroken, though the shoe might well be on the other foot.

The memory of my mother telling the story that I'll shortly relate floated to the surface of my oxygen-deprived brain several times during my hospital stay. The first such occasion coincided with the floor nurse's questioning of my report of multiple broken bones so soon after my blithely answering "no" to the question, "is anyone you love hurting you." Rather than perpetuate her clear suspicion of He Who Adores Me, (he who was not even in my life during most of the breaks), I allowed her to slap a bright yellow "Fall Risk" band on my arm, and I endured three days of indignities from people half my age and a quarter as resilient as I believe I have proven myself to be, awkward gait and all.

My mother's voice rose in my head, chagrin-laced, regretful, for the tone she reportedly found herself using with her "clinic patients," a tone that she admitted arose from her middle-class assumptions: *You are poor, therefore you must be stupid. You are in a wheelchair, therefore you must be deaf.* Even my mother, liberal, Democrat, war-protesting, fell prey to such sad truisms.

The morning after my admission, the day shift had its turn at humiliating me. I discovered, to my horror, that being a fall risk in the heart unit meant having one's bed rigged to blare if one set one's dainty, bare toes upon the cold laminate floor for purposes of traversing a few feet to attend to one's morning personal tasks. An over-sized, thunderous aide appeared to scold me and grab for my elbow. As any person with an "awkward gait" will attest, grabbing for one's elbow triggers a sudden jar which sends you tottering in the opposite direction of the grabber, and so I nearly became the falling patient that their precautions ostensibly intended to forestall. *Let go of me!* I cried, desperate for the bathroom but determined to get there with as little humiliation as possible.

The nurse appeared beside my torturer. *Darling, darling,* she bellowed -- or cooed, perhaps, but by this time, I had no tolerance for such appellations, and I heard her voice as loud enough to wake my eternally sleeping maternal unit. *Darling, honey, we have to help you, you're a fall risk.*

I stood by the sink, just about ready to slam the door in her face. First of all, I spat out. *I am not your darling. Second, I am not a fall risk.* I only admitted to falling on the rare occasion to keep your night-shift counter-part from assuming that my history of broken bones should be attributed to my husband beating me. *I've been disabled longer than you have been alive, and, really, it is rude to call someone you've never even met, 'Darling'.*

My mother's voice, telling her story, the story that I am

about to share with you, drifted up to the surface in my consciousness. I glared at the nurse, who stared back with a quiet intensity. I could see her thinking of how to keep me, whom she perceived as a nearly rabid patient, from posing a risk both to her calm day and my admittedly very sick self. I saw the precise moment when she realized that she had let her assumptions guide her tone, in that condescending us-or-them way of medical professionals, even well-intended medical professionals, even excellent, caring and concerned medical professionals.

Like my mother.

Who walked one day, down the hallway, a few feet from her EKG department, at the now-defunct St. Louis County Hospital. Clinic patients awaited her, and you should read "clinic patients" to mean people who were too poor to get their EKGs in the offices of private doctors, and so were forced to report to my mother's office to suffer the indignity of removing their upper garments behind a flimsy curtain in a room which also held filing cabinets and desks at which my mother and her colleagues did their work.

Stop me if you've heard this one. It's a favorite story of mine.

A man approached my mother and ask for directions to the laboratory. My mother eagerly responded, trying to be helpful. In a loud voice, gesturing, she told him: *Okay, the lab. You walk down the hall. Way, way down the hall. You pass an office that looks like the lab but it is NOT the lab, it is the blood bank. DON'T GO IN THERE. Go past that place and keep going down the hall. Way, way, way down the hall, really far, and then you come to a set of DOORS.*

The man look intently at her. He replied, *Doors? You mean, those things with knobs?*

My mother quickly corrected him. *Oh, no! These doors DO NOT HAVE KNOBS. These are SWINGING DOORS.* And then she saw the stethoscope around his neck.

As the short blond nurse stood silent in front of me, re-evaluating her prior notions of what I must be -- changing me from a faceless "fall risk" to a human being who has beaten all odds and clings desperately to her notion of self-sufficiency, I thought of my mother, and of the lesson she learned, all those years ago, about assumptions. And here we were, this nurse and I, making assumptions about each other. I assumed that she called me "darling" because she thought I was demented. And she assumed that because I have suffered multiple, small and annoying breaks from time to time when the earth arose to insult my gait-challenged legs, I could not walk from the bed to the bathroom without an attendant. Yes, yes, I know: Policy, procedure; rules, regulations; liabilities and laws. But still -- the assumptions had flared and had bitten us both in the butt.

We reached a compromise, the nurse and I. She did not require me to have an attendant hold onto me, or to wear those ridiculous, loose-fitting socks, or to wear a gait belt. I agreed to advise the CNA when I wanted to move around, and to let them at least be in the room. The bed alarm would only be activated after 10 p.m. She would call me "Corinne." Nobody would grab my arm.

I heard my mother chuckling, shifting in her grave, and settling back, ready to let another memory rise to the surface, as needed, to teach her daughter another life lesson, on some other day, in some other place, when I would again need her wisdom.

Mugwumpishly tendered,


Corinne Corley

# Saturday Musings, 14 April 2012

Good morning,

The trill of a recorder, a flute perhaps, wafts from the radio during a story on NPR. Morning drifts into mid-day, and I lounge in my gray cotton nightgown, thick socks on my feet, coffee cooling at my elbow.

It's been a dicey week. I've seen daybreak from an alarmed hospital bed at week's beginning, and nightfall with an inhaler inches from my elbow at week's end. I've quit a client; taken in new ones; shared stories of survival; listened to whispered tales of struggle from the pursed lips of a suffering friend. I survived Friday the Thirteenth. I lived.

In the throes of the wickedness of an asthma relapse, I abandoned work for a day or three, and immersed myself in books. I bought a new pair of shoes on E-bay and learned how to use a modern, sleek Nebulizer. I helped a friend understand documents from an estate in which she is named as an heir; I proofed my son's resume, marveling at his accomplishments which I had never seen paraded one after another in black-and-white; and I made friends with a pharmacy technician who shares my frightening, breath-taking ailment.

And last night, I dreamed of my grandmother. I walked again with her down South Sixth Street, in Springfield, Illinois, in new penny loafers that she purchased at the shoe store next to the Sonotone House of Hearing where she and my grandfather tested hearing and sold hearing aids. I held her hand, listening to her tell me to put my best foot forward. I tilted my head back, again, letting my curls fall down my back, and, again, asked her which foot is that, Nana? Again, as she had so many decades ago, she gazed down on my face with sparkling eyes, set in pale Austrian skin, and in a gentle voice with just a lilting trace of her immigrant's accent, assured me that my best foot was the one striking the sidewalk in front of me, first left, first right, then left, then right, and on until we reached Strong's and the waitress set a steaming plate of stewed chicken in front of us.

Neither of us then knew that I had asthma; or would some time in life develop asthma; or that I would later in life find out that I am allergic to the swirls of thick rich honey that the restaurant stirred into their softened butter for us to smear on thick, hot biscuits.

She held my hand in hers and walked with pride down the street that she owned, nodding to tradesmen; gently pulling me to a stop at cross-walks, nudging me forward when the light turned green. And after lunch, she released me into the back room of my grandparents' business, where they kindly stored books for the bookstore next door. There my world expanded, as I sat amidst the stacks of novels, and encyclopedias, and volumes about how to care for your pet, or your parent, or your garden. Sometimes I fell asleep sitting on a carton of books, with the *Wind and the Willows* clutched in my sticky hands, and *Anne of Greene Gables* under my small head with its great mass of brownish red curls carefully cultivated around a nest of clothes pins each night by my grandmother, in those summer days when I stayed with her, long ago, before I knew what my life would give me.

Mugwumpishly tendered,


Corinne Corley

# Saturday Musings, 23 April 2011

Good morning,

A wave of color catches my attention each time I turn my head. I recently acquired a temporary prism on my right glasses lens, which raised the number of corrective prisms from 3 to 9. As a consequence, I feel as though I have consumed just enough intoxicating beverages to be tipsy, feeling faintly nauseous; and the world shimmies.

Growing old might well surpass the alternative in desirability, but not because of how easy I find it. Ah, life.

Spring surrounds me, with its nippy air, and the bright, verdant expanse of lawn. The Japanese maple raises its delicate tendrils towards the pale stretch of the clean sky. My world shakes itself, rising from the fog of hibernation.

In recent conversations, I have had to confront the coming religious holiday and this morning, as it looms, I discover that I have fewer ties to Christianity than I thought possible. In the past, I have been able to ignore the religious celebrations and focus on honoring the turning of the seasons and our commitment to a fresh start.

I think about my mother's last Easter. Cold gripped St. Louis. Her backyard still looked barren, with only a few brave flowers nudging themselves above the frost line. She had lost her hair to chemotherapy, and wore a tri-corner scarf over the smoothness of her skull, perhaps to keep out the cold, perhaps to save her grandchildren from the fright of her grim appearance. She sat on a park bench and watched the children hunt for eggs -- Lisa, Rick and Cate, in their church clothes, with serious looks as they concentrated on the search. I sat beside my mother and held her hand from time to time. I caught her glancing sideways with annoyance, and let her fingers slip from my grasp.

Later that day, after my siblings had helped to wash the dishes, and my mother and I sat at the breakfast room table in the quiet of the empty house, my mother searched my face with her warm brown eyes. Not finding an answer, she inquired, in gentle tones, if anything was wrong. *Oh, not much,* I replied. *Only that my mother is dying, that's no big deal.* I pushed back my chair and snatched at our tea cups, moving without grace into the kitchen while she sat, alone, in the darkening room. I might as well have slapped her face.

I came back and lowered myself into the chair, and looked down at her worn hands, resting on the surface of the wooden table. She moved, slightly, slowly until one of her fingers rested on my arm. The weight of her illness hung in the chilly air of the evening, in the silence which surrounded us. I fidgeted beneath her gaze, resisting the comfort that she wanted me to take from her own acceptance of her fate. Easter Sunday, 1985, and I was not quite 30. My mother would not see her next birthday, and my boyfriend and I would end our relationship a few days after her funeral. He only stayed for my sake, to help me through. By Christmas, my grandfather would have died, and I would have slipped into a pattern of drinking, carousing, and forgetting to go to work.

I don't know if she foresaw my decline in that moment. She reached further over, to place her hand on my shoulder. *It's going to be okay,* she told me, in the soft tones that only a mother can use. But I did not believe her, and I slumped against the chair, falling into my misery, while the sun set outside my childhood home, and my father watched television in the living room.

The house around me has grown quiet. In a little while, I will start to clean the house. I will send the dog out into the yard, where clumps of grass surround the wild violets. I've bought good chocolate, and I have chosen a dress to wear to church tomorrow. There is a slight chill in the air, but spring has taken hold, with a stubborn, cheerful insistence that I might do well to emulate.

Mugwumpishly tendered,


Corinne Corley

# Saturday Musings, 25 April 2015

Good morning,

The rain had not yet started when I descended the stairs to the first floor and let the dog outside. Now it patters on the wood of the deck and the dog has retreated inside her house. She will not be persuaded to venture up to the kitchen to come inside. I am left to be amused and watch the rain from the front door, stretching my tired limbs, shaking my head at the feelings coursing through me. Another day, another chance to wonder: *Is this medicine working? If so, then why do I still feel so sick?*

I see the American flag on my house and smile, suddenly, without inhibition. A light shines on this flag -- a floodlight that we included in the new porch design both to light the steps and to allow us to fly the flag without interruption. For the same reason, we replace our flag nearly every year, most recently in 2013 with a quality, sewn all-weather flag. Many have doubted my patriotism: I have never served; I do not advocate war; I question the way our country has been managed. But drive past my home and you will see that I proudly display our nation's most visible and beloved symbol.

Standing here reminds me of a rainy day nearly fifty years ago -- forty-seven? -- when I spent the summer at Camp Fire Girls camp on a "poor girl's scholarship." As the memory floats to the surface, I give myself to it.

Among our troop were twins, Barbara and Bonnie Cross, whose mother led us. Barbara and Bonnie looked alike but in reality, could have been strangers. Bonnie leaned toward more typically feminine deportment while Barbara played sports and had strong, sturdy limbs. I liked Bonnie but I admired Barbara the most. I yearned for her approval and attention.

A group of us occupied a rustic portion of the camp, sleeping not in cabins but in three-sided bays with crude roofs and a canvas flap for rain protection. Iron bunks, three sets to a structure, and thin mattresses contributed to the military feel of the place. This group consisted mostly of experienced campers, twelve years old or so, and we did not have to participate in the daily ritual of the place. We hiked, boated, swam, and learned about survival.

Though I fit the age, I had only been to camp once before that summer and did not fit the profile of an experienced attendee. I struggled to keep pace. Barb Cross thrived on the rigors of this schedule. But with my clumsy legs and pale skin, I caught poison ivy, grew blisters, and lay in bed each night aching in every muscle.

Toward the end of the week, our troop would be leading a hike through "unmapped land". No one told us what we would find. We would be following markers through brambles, over boulders, with only a rudimentary path beneath our feet. Barb Cross could not contain her excitement nor I my dread.

We stood in the rain one day for the process of grouping ourselves in pairs for the next day's hike. I looked and felt miserable as the others jostled together, laughing about the rain's causing their hair to frizz, guessing whether we'd hike if the rain did not stop, pairing off while I stood forlornly by myself. No one wanted me, not even a pretty girl from Springfield with whom I had become friends. But Barb Cross stepped forward to choose me and then she did an even more unthinkable act: She volunteered the two of us to rise at dawn, go to the place where the trail-blazing would occur, and use our compasses and a map of the area to mark the trail that the others would later follow.

I lay awake that night until no sound drifted to me from others sleeping in adjacent bunks. I could not imagine why Barbara chose me except from pity. I would slow her progress; I would fall; I would doom our task and cause her to be humiliated in front of the several participating troops and the camp leaders. I fell asleep with silent tears streaming down my cheeks, their saltiness stinging my chapped lips.

I slid out of the building in the morning, dressed in slacks and the only shoes I owned. I had tied my braid with a Camp Fire Girls kerchief and stashed a few supplies in a small pack. I pulled aside the canvas and peered out: the rain had gone, leaving behind cool sweet air and a gentle freshness. I stepped down, steadying myself on the unpaved bare ground.

Barbara waited for me, a stout backpack beside her, in which she had stowed the red flags that she and I would tie on branches to guide the others who came later. She carried an ax. I shuddered when I saw it. But I forced myself to remain composed as we moved toward the road.

Barbara had the map provided by the counselors. She took us across a clearing and into the woods, where we found an initial, large red flag which told us where to start the trail. Then Barbara moved past it, wielding the little hatchet at the spindly new growth of trees. I followed her, tying red cloth to the young trees every few feet, dodging to avoid being slapped by the branches whipped away by Barbara's strong arms.

After we had gone a hundred feet, Barbara stopped and looked back at the narrow clearing that her efforts had created. Fire rose in her eyes as she surveyed the path down which the other girls in the group would come. They would not have to do much to navigate the way; she had done more than the leaders expected. She glanced at me and grinned, then resumed her forward trek. The sun crept higher. Sweat rose on my forehead but I kept going.

72

I fell a few times. Barbara immediately dropped her pack and came back to me, gently lifting me from the floor of the woods and brushing debris from my back. Each time, she stayed until I found my footing again, then moved away, retrieved her backpack and ax, and started forward again. She moved farther ahead of me as I tired, but we both kept going, Barbara working the compass and the map, me just following Barb, tying red strips of fabric every four or five feet, feeling the burn in my chest.

I don't know how far our efforts took us, but suddenly, we broke through the forest to another clearing. This one stood on the edge of a lovely ravine. We crossed the clearing and looked down. What we beheld could not be called a canyon but it certainly took our breath away as surely as the deepest gorge. Barbara let out a grand laugh and threw her arms around me. *We did it!* she cried. *We made it! We did it! You and me! Not those other girls! You and me!* We fell on the ground, laughing, congratulating each other, even though in my heart, I knew that but for Barbara, I would have failed and turned away in desolation.

Later that day, we followed the rest of the girls as they made their way through the forest using our red flags as guides. They widened the path, cleared the brush created by their efforts, trampled down undergrowth so that eventually, even the youngest campers could walk that way. When the group of us broke through the woods to the clearing by the ravine, we discovered that a picnic had been laid, with portable tables, coolers, chairs, and food. Our troop leaders awaited us.

But Barbara and I walked past the impromptu party to stand together on the edge of the ravine, looking down at the rocks, the straggly trees, and the floor of the ravine with its small stream and untamed growth. We did not speak. The sun shone full upon us. I felt a sense of peace flow through me. I don't know if Barbara shared that sensation but a few minutes later, she touched my arm. I looked at her. A smile rose on her face and I felt my own face relax beneath her gaze. And then, still without speaking, we turned away, and went to join the others.

That evening, Barbara and I paired again for the nightly flag-lowering ceremony. She worked the ropes with her strong arms, to slowly lower the flag while Taps sounded throughout the camp. I stood beside the pole, gathering the end of the flag. She took the opposite end as it came down, and gently unhooked the flag. She walked away, stretching the flag straight, then methodically moved towards me, carefully holding the flag taut so it would not touch the ground. Barbara folded the flag in the manner that our leaders had taught us, moving closer and closer to where I stood, until the last fold. She neatly tucked the end to keep the flag in form until it would be hung at Reveille the next morning. Then she held the flag reverently in her extended arms, again, as we had been taught. We walked towards the main building while the last notes of Taps played and the sun set.

Mugwumpishly tendered.


Corinne Corley

# Saturday Musings, 05 May 2012

Good morning,

My old Mac balances on the metal table on our lovely deck. My hair lifts and sways across my face in the gentle morning breeze. I hear birds joyfully greeting the rising spring sun. My gaze falls on the new landscaping next door, and the burst of colorful blooms in the pots on my porch.

I would have to google -- if I may use that as a lower-case verb without incurring a summons -- the history of Cinco de Mayo, but I do know that today will be honored with many celebrations, including Paddy Murphy, a gala event of my son's fraternity (SAE). In downtown Kansas City's Power and Light District, it is Derby Day. At the Holmes House here in Brookside, I am celebrating Clean Out the Closet Day, a semi-annual event that stirs my soul and provides bounty for local thrift stores, in this case, the Hope Chest, which raises money for several causes, including the VALA Gallery. Besides the boon to charity, I derive major satisfaction from an orderly closet.

The seasons change as the world keeps spinning. I dodged another bullet this week, once again receiving undeserved bounty from the Universe, where my stock rises and falls according to my own folly. I took a nasty fall last Sunday but Thursday learned I had not damaged my artificial joint. The bad news? The pain in my knee stems from a bone-on-metal situation which can only be remedied by surgery. I weigh the odds of clotting and the potential of spending two months without income against the inconvenience of sleepless nights and the increasing need for pain medication. A toss up, as far as I can tell.

As Mother's Day draws near, I think of my own mother and feel the pain of her loss as though it had happened just yesterday. I suppose time heals most wounds, but overcoming the loss of one's parent might require as many decades as you had their love. A friend watched her mother fade last week, and I feel the freshness of her agony and wish I could help. But I have found, and she will find, that the only helpful words echo in her own heart spoken in her mother's voice, consisting of the many lessons she imparted, and the many avowals of dedication she whispered over the years.

I also learned this week that my son will be in Los Angeles all summer. I had been expecting, even hoping for this news. I got it virtually, by way of a forwarded electronic mail from the company that has chosen him as their summer intern. I've yet to learn whether it will be paid or unpaid but it doesn't matter, because it will provide him both experience and contacts in the world in which he hopes to work after graduation next year. One step closer to independence; one step further from the nest. A friend asked if I am sad that he won't be here, and I can honestly answer, *no,* because 'not here' provides what he wants and needs. I had him for twenty years. Any pain that I experience in his absence pales next to the brilliance of his accomplishments and his own satisfaction in them.

I hear sirens wailing to the east -- fire trucks, an ambulance, police cars -- their blaring urgency sending motorists skittering to the side of the road. The noise recedes as it grows distant and I find myself making a little sign of the cross on my chest, an old habit that has died hard, one that invites the God of Catholicism to send angels to watch over those at the other end of the ambulance's journey. I glance around the porch, suspicious that I've been caught in this relapse into the symbolism of my childhood religion. Only the old girl cat watches me, and with such disinterest that my sheepishness fades into laughter.

Saturday looms empty and welcoming. And as the day wanes, I will begin to think about dinner, and my returning husband, and what Sunday holds. For now, though, I will pour another cup of Eight O'clock coffee, and spread open the Kansas City Star, for my daily session of yelling at writers who have forgotten the rules of grammar.

Mugwumpishly tendered,


Corinne Corley

# Saturday Musings, 07 May 2011

Good morning,

Danger alerts sound outside: dogs bark, birds start a frantic twittering. Intruders pass -- a young mother with a stroller; a prissy little poodle, walked by a broad-shouldered man with a bald head. I don't look out the window, but I recognize the noise made by the three dogs at the side of our house -- mine and the neighbors' two -- and I imagine the morning brigade. Saturday in Brookside. I continue reading my paper, drinking my coffee, listening with half an ear to the soundtrack of my life.

I'm rushing myself a bit; I'm distracted by the knowledge that the number of coffee cups accumulated on the floor of my Saturn has started to affect my gas mileage, as has the heavy layer of road dirt on its exterior. I cannot think of any more excuses for avoiding this chore, so I'll grab a pair of jeans and my heavy shoes, and spend a half hour pumping quarters into the do-it-yourself car wash, holding the heavy wand with my right hand, babying my left wrist which still smarts from a recent sprain.

I used to take better care of my vehicles. My first car shone with endless rounds of wax that I rubbed into its British Racing Green surface. An MG Midget, in which I felt chic and fashionable. In a photograph album somewhere, in a box, in my basement, my eighteen-year-old self gazes out from its driver's seat. The top is folded back; the wind, doubtless, plays on my face. I wear shades in the picture, back in the days when I could still correct my vision with contact lenses -- the hard kind, for which one often had to search on one's hands and knees, on the tiled floor of the bathroom. In that decades-old snapshot, I have a bandanna tied over my tangle of long, curly hair and I wear a blue-jean jacket. I've got my arm dangling over the door, the other hand touching the steering wheel, and a broad smile widens my mouth.

The summer after my second year of college, I dated a police officer who worked second shift, ending his duty after eleven o'clock, when he would rap on my apartment door after parking his vehicle in the underground garage of my building. On one such night, he arrived well after midnight, and as I opened the door, he remarked, *When I saw your car wasn't there, I figured you got tired of waiting and went out with somebody else.* I shuddered as he spoke the words, and pushed past him, running down the interior stairwell, bursting through the garage entrance, standing, shocked, in front of my assigned space, in which I had parked my car earlier that evening.

My friend came up behind me, softly, putting his hand on my arm. *I'll call it in,* he said. I nodded, without speaking.

They found the car, stripped of its wiring, several miles from my apartment. My brothers installed a fuel-line kill switch when they replaced the wiring harness. Periodically, I would come down and discover it had been taken again. I would set out walking, dangling the keys, and find it a block or two away, the farthest it could be driven on the gas left in the line. Hot-wired, taken, and then abandoned.

I burned the clutch out on that MG three times before I finally gave it to my brother and bought a Chevy Nova from my cousin Angela. I took the Nova with me to Kansas City, when I moved here in 1980 for law school. The first summer, its carburetor rebelled and the car kept stalling; the guys at the Montgomery Ward Auto Center couldn't figure out what was wrong. I bought a carburetor rebuild kit and a Polaroid camera. I took the thing apart in the parking lot at the shopping center, piece by piece, photographing it as I went. Then I rebuilt it, using the line of pictures as my guide. When I finished, the vehicle started on the first try, and I wiped my hands, threw away the trash, and went home.

I sold that Nova for more than I had paid for it, and bought a big Oldsmobile which talked to me. *The door is ajar,* it said, in an insipid female voice. *Fasten your seat belt,* she admonished me. *Oh, shut up,* I took to telling her, before I figured out which fuse ran her and pulled it to silence her. The transmission went out on the Olds and she went for scrap, just before the accident which crushed my leg and netted me enough from my Uninsured Motorist provision to buy my first new car, a Nissan Sentra. I drove that little wagon until 1990, then gave it to a law student who worked for my firm in Fayetteville. I bought an old Audi with a sunroof until I drove until I returned to Kansas City to manage a Congressional campaign and had to dump the German car to appease the UAW contingent.

In the last decade, I've had three Buick Centuries, a small Saturn with manually operated windows, and a Chevy Blazer that introduced me to the world of SUV drivers, a world that just seems safer. Now I drive a Vue, and I'm hoping to get a sweet new Buick Enclave some day.

I can step through my life on the roofs of the cars that I have owned. I never expected to care about something so seemingly trivial, but I find that I am nostalgic for the little MG Midget with its classic lines and traditional paint job. I long to reclaim the casual air with which I shifted gears, as I accelerated into third on the highway between my mother's home in North St. Louis County and the dingy streets of the city where I lived. I have studied the face of the girl in the photo, her head thrown back, her eyes shielded but surely wild with laughter, her smile radiant. I do not know where she went, that girl; and I wonder what I have in common with her.

The house has assumed a deserted air with the departure of most of its human occupants. The cat yowls for water, no doubt standing on the edge of the sink in the downstairs bathroom. I tear my gaze back to the present, and swallow the last cold coffee. I rise from my chair, and the world shifts to a forward spin, while outside my home, the barking of my dog diminishes, and the startled birds fall silent.

Mugwumpishly tendered,


Corinne Corley

# Saturday Musings, 14 May 2011

Good morning,

Our schizophrenic weather staggered back into winter this morning, though the Saturday morning tennis players wore their customary white shorts as they whistled their way to their cars and wandered off, leaving me to shiver and huddle over a chilling cup of bad coffee. Weak light streams into my bedroom through the tilted slats of the blinds, falling onto the faded, tangled black lace of my grandmother's shawl.

The sight of this shawl reminds me of the time that I first wore it, at a party given by me and my college roommates. We all wore black lace dresses and heavy jewelry, old Hollywood hair-styles and shiny sling-back sandals. We posed for our portrait on the stairway to the upstairs of our Laclede Town townhouse, heads thrown back, varying degrees of vibrancy on our faces. I stand on the bottom step, in a tea-length dress with a wide skirt, capped sleeves and scooped neckline. I am not smiling; but my eyes squarely caught the camera's lens. I cannot tell what I was thinking.

At the end of that party, the three of us pushed the chairs back against the walls. I listlessly vacuumed crumbs from the carpet while someone carried beer cans and Margarita glasses to the kitchen. Outside, the night air began to yield to the rising sun, and the first glimmer of Sunday morning noises rose from the street -- the heavy ramble of the newspaper truck, a last, desperate siren's wail, the beckoning of a church bell. When we had finished cleaning, we shed our finery in favor of flannel, and crawled into our respective beds, with curtains drawn against the brightness of the morning light.

I awakened that day long after noon, though the house remained silent and my roommates' doors still had not opened. I softly padded down the stairs, and pulled the coffee-maker from its cubby under a cabinet. As I waited for the brewing process to be completed, I pushed the furniture back into its customary configuration.

With my coffee clutched closely to my chest, I slid the patio doors open, and stepped outside. The vague chill of a spring afternoon kissed my face and I closed my eyes, sipping coffee, receiving the grace of the wind's caress.

A woman's voice startled me, and I nearly dropped my mug. *You all had one heck of a party last night,* she said, softly. I turned towards the patio next to ours, regarding the slender form of my neighbor, who sat on a low stool with a small child leaning against her body. We had not met. When the three of us had rented our place, the entire row had been unoccupied. *I didn't know anybody lived there now,* I told the woman. *I'm sorry; did we disturb you?*

She turned away, wrapping one arm around the child's small frame, gazing across her patio to the abutting edge of the yards behind ours. She shrugged. *Not really,* she admitted. *This one don't sleep too good, since his daddy left.*

I set my cup down on the small metal table between our two lawn chairs. *Do you want some coffee,* I asked the woman, and when she accepted, I stepped into the kitchen and then returned with a mug for her, and a glass of juice for her son. She took both with a tiny nod and the briefest of smiles below her somber eyes. I sat down on the chair closest to her and the boy, and for a few minutes, no one spoke.

The child broke the uneasy silence. *This is good,* he whispered, and his mother's body jerked, just briefly, as though in fear. *Thank you, honey,* I offered, putting as much sincerity into my reply as I could. Silence resumed.

When the little boy had consumed all of his orange juice, he slid from between his mother's bony knees and handed his glass to me. *Thank you for my breakfast,* he said, solemnly, carefully, before returning to the woman's side.

My neighbor rose, then, and placed her empty coffee cup beside mine on the table. She swung the boy high into her arms, and spared me another small bend of her head. Without further comment, she carried her son into her own house. As the door slid closed, before the beige drapes blocked my view, I glimpsed a scattering of cardboard boxes, a few bulging black trash bags, and a tiny, lonely pile of broken toys.

From within my apartment, I heard sounds of my roommates rummaging in our kitchen. One called to the other as they debated whether they would have breakfast or dinner. Someone spoke to me, and I pulled my gaze away from the wrinkled expanse of fabric covering the neighbor's patio door. *Coming!* I responded, and hauled myself up from the chair, scooping all three cups from the table, tossing a little cold coffee onto the bare ground between our patio and the one next door.

From time to time, over the next few months, I would see the woman leaving for work and bid her good morning. The child walked beside her, usually with a tiny backpack settled between his shoulder blades, and a grimy stuffed bear held in the crook of his arm. Neither of them spoke to me in those brief encounters, although the child often let his eyes slip sideways to meet mine, and occasionally he flashed a hurried, radiant smile, to let me know that he still remembered the taste of the cold, sweet juice.

We broke housekeeping at the end of the school year. I moved out last, and whatever man I was dating at the time hauled my belongings for me, backing his pick-up truck as close to the entry of the apartment as he could. We loaded it with an odd assortment of storage containers and suitcases, the bookshelf my great-grandfather made, my old bed frame, and a couple of boxes of books. We bundled the last of the rubbish to be taken to the dumpster. As we finished cleaning, I noticed that the front door of the town house next to ours stood open. I stepped across to the stoop, and peered into the living room.

It took a few minutes to realize that the place was entirely empty, with no sign of the woman or her son. No boxes, no bags, no broken toys. No furniture. Nothing. I stood, surveying the barren look of the place, astonished that I could have been as oblivious to their departure as I had been to their initial arrival.

After a few minutes, my boyfriend honked the horn, impatient to get the load to my new apartment before sundown. I shrugged, to no one in particular, and closed the doors of both houses, making sure the locks clicked. Then I left, without a backwards glance.

Mugwumpishly tendered,


Corinne Corley

# Saturday Musings, 29 May 2010

Good morning,

A vigorous chorus of birds dragged me into awakening. I have made a passable pot of coffee, and sip from a heavy white mug, still smiling at my recent discovery that a well-intentioned house-sitter had inadvertently switched positions of the canisters on my counter so that I unknowingly had been decaffeinated this week.

I can report that my body struggled with the resultant fatigue; I found myself napping in the evening and canceling social engagements with the thought that I must surely be coming down with something. I am amused; but I firmly resituated the containers so as to insure that we would not again be poisoned with the innocuousness of the decaf beans.

The customary calmness of my dwelling has been dispelled by the return of the prodigal son. The piano sounds beneath his nimble fingers; the chords of Bach's Suite No. 1 for cello stream from his Les Paul. He unpacked with alarming speed on Sunday, filling three trash bags full of the clothes left behind in his dresser last fall, saying that his taste has changed, he will not again wear these clothes, sorry, Mom.

I am not sorry. I smile. He has matured, and I have no problem with the thought that his once-loved baggy jeans will grace the frame of another mother's miracle.

Yesterday, Patrick and I helped gather trappings to hang "The Potter's Hand", a new display at the VALA Gallery. We scoured area stores for large pieces of cloth to use as drapes, and our journey took us to the Salvation Army Family Store, just up Johnson Drive from the Gallery.

As I walked down the linens aisle, a soft, hesitant voice called from behind me.

*Lady, excuse me, lady.*

I turned, and beheld a tall, sturdy woman, with an armful of children's clothing, clutching a battered top-bound spiral notebook in one hand. I stopped, summoning a smile. I did not recognize her, but I knew the look on her face. Since I myself have often worn that peculiar blend of need and determination, I could do nothing but respond.

*Excuse me,* she repeated. *Do you have CP?*

I have not been asked that question in a long time, and I certainly did not expect to be asked that question in the middle of a May afternoon, in Mission, Kansas, in the comparative complacency of my middle age. But I think I smiled, and replied that I did not, and I think I did so without rancor.

Her face sagged, inspiring my eyebrows to lift and my curiosity to rise just as much. She satisfied my unspoken question without hesitation.

*My daughter has CP,* she told me. *I am always on the look-out for role models for her, and there was something about you -- I thought -- you looked ---*

--- In the small space of time between the trailing of her sentence and the moment when I found my voice, I sailed into the distant past.

I closed my eyes, just briefly, not long enough to startle her, I hope. I heard again the derisive voices of a gaggle of boys from my parish school. I beheld again their wildly stumbling progress, a half-block behind me, on West Florissant Avenue, one Sunday when my mother and I walked home from church the long way. My mother stopped, stunned. I put my small hand on her arm, urging her forward. Don't look back, I told her *It's worse if you say anything.* I continued to trudge towards home, my Brogues slapping against the pavement, my knees bobbing with unsightly grace within the folds of my cotton dress.

*Do they always do that?* she said, in tender tones.

*Yes, pretty much,* I replied. *Unless Mark and Kevin are with me.* My big brothers.

Beneath her steady, unfathomable gaze, I tossed my head, two long braids floating over my shoulder. I had no faith in the power of an adult to squelch the teasing. In the warm summer air, my skin grew clammy and I felt a long shudder course through me. I closed my eyes and barreled forward, away from their taunts, away from the awkward bent of their bodies in imitation.

I had gone another ten yards or so before I opened my eyes, realizing that my mother no longer kept pace with my careening gait. I turned, and saw that she had gone back to face the small gang of ten-year-olds. I could not move. I could only watch; I could only listen.

Beneath the onslaught of her scolding, the little hoodlums dispersed, some south to the blocks of subdivision houses known as Country Club Hills; some north, into Jennings proper. My mother returned to my side, taking hold of my thin arm with her strong hand, setting me once more in motion. She shifted her pocketbook on her shoulder, and smoothed her skirt.

*Come on,* she said. *Your father will be waiting for breakfast.*

She said no more, nor did I. The heavy pall that had overtaken my body eased; the air around me again felt pleasant and the breeze again rose to cool me. I stole a glance at the strong profile of my mother's Arab heritage, at the liquid brownness of her eyes and the bold crook of her nose, so unlike my own pale blueness and little Irish button. As we rounded the corner at the end of our block, she threw her own head back with a sharp snap, her mouth set, her brow furrowed, and I wondered what she was thinking, but did not ask.

In the closeness of the thrift store yesterday, I studied another mother's face. There it is, I told myself. That look. I've seen that look. My heart swelled, and I stopped, in earnest now; and we spoke about her daughter; two years old and the victim of a neonatal stroke that killed her identical twin. I had some ideas for her; the life I have led has given me many obstacles to overcome along with many examples of others who have done so with more finesse than I. As she groped in her vinyl handbag, I pulled a pen from my own purse to hand her, and she took it with an earnest carelessness.

She wrote down what I recounted: the URL of a website at which she could listen to a recent NPR interview with a doctor doing research on strokes in small children; lists of local services that could help her daughter which I have discovered during my years doing work with Children's Services. She talked a little then, describing the child, in tones both poignant and proud. As our conversation unfolded, the hubbub of other shoppers swirled around us, within which, I swore, I could hear my mother's voice.

Mugwumpishly tendered,


Corinne Corley

# Saturday Musings, 02 June 2012

Good morning,

At hand on the table stands a china cup filled with an Americano. A Nutty Girl sandwich provides my breakfast. In a week filled with happenings, I forgot to buy groceries, get coffee, and pick up my prescriptions. In addition to a successful quarterly art opening at my professional suite, the last seven days held something that distracted me in a way that any mother will understand: My son drove three days cross-country to spend the summer in Los Angeles.

His traveling companion, Alex Thompson, arrived Monday evening from Lexington. Alex's reputation as an accommodating friend preceded him by several hours, when Patrick and I discussed whether to cook dinner at home or go to a restaurant. He told me that whatever we did would be fine: *Alex is agreeable, Mom, and I'm malleable, so you pick.* We went to a Japanese restaurant, and, astonishingly, Alex not only enjoyed himself but actually made a friend. Our waitress hailed from Louisville and went to high school with people whom Alex had known.

It's a small world.

On Tuesday morning, both of their cars loaded and the gas tanks filled, a cooler stocked with snacks and sandwiches, coffee mugs beside them and water bottles at hand, Alex and Patrick took to the highway. They each hugged me, as I stood on our steps, heart in my throat, trying to look brave. I thought about my son's trepidation over the last several weeks, while he waited to hear from the agent for whom he hoped to be interning and the management company through which Alex's family had arranged for the two of them to sublet. Before the confirming emails hit our inboxes, on a morning two or three days before their scheduled departure, he confided that he had had a sort of recurring waking nightmare that both fell through, and he found himself unemployed and homeless in L.A.

Both internship and sublet arranged, and Alex's career set to launch, the two of them prepared to caravan across the country. But just before they slipped behind their respective steering wheels, Alex handed me a CD. Patrick made this for you last night, he told me, and I saw, in my son's writing, a single word written on the compact disc: *Graceland.*

Many things separate my son and me: his nature is calm, where mine rises to the Type A level; he stands by his beliefs but instinctively tolerates those of others, a wise choice with which I still struggle; he defaults to sweet and serene, at least outwardly, where I incline to defensive prickliness. But we share a love of music, and in particular certain artists, including Ladysmith Black Mambazo, a male vocal group whose strong, serene voices flavor the *Graceland* album.

When I left for work an hour or so after the travelers departed, I slipped the CD into the player in my Saturn. By the time I hit the Plaza, I had played "Diamonds in the Soles of Her Shoes" twice, my head and hands keeping time to the amusement of drivers in adjacent cars at stop lights. As I drove up Broadway, and rounded the corner at 40th street to make the dog-leg to my customary parking space in front of our building, I hit the track selection button to find my favorite. The haunting lyrics of Ladysmith Black Mambazo singing Paul Simon's "Homeless" filled my car.

And at the turn, with the voices of these singers from South Africa flooding my car, my eyes raised to the sight of the Revolution Church, on whose sidewalk a gathering of lonely souls collects each morning, waiting for the soup kitchen to open.

They stood, in twos, or threes, wearing layers of clothing that seemed senseless in the heat of our early summer. Some sat apart, on the curb. All had clutches of belongings beside them, or tucked between their feet. None of the men were clean-shaven. Most seemed dirtier than I would ever find comfortable. And as the harmony spilled out into the street through my open windows, the eyes of the men and women waiting outside the church turned toward my vehicle.

Ten hours from that point in time, my son and Alex would check into a fifty-six dollar hotel in Aurora, Colorado, and nosh on the sandwiches I had prepared for them. Later, after surveying their Facebook friends for dinner suggestions, they would find a Ruby Tuesday's. On the evening of the second day, they would learn what "next services 100 miles" might mean to them, and that evening, they would enter the Castle Valley, Utah, home of my oldest friend in all the world, and talk until midnight about peregrines and life, flicking cardboard into the chiminea on her flagstone patio, sleeping in her small home beneath her lofted bedroom, drinking from a spring-fed water system and using a chemical toilet. On the third day, they would deal with over-aggressive cruise control on my son's Blazer that would trick us all into thinking his transmission had failed, and, finally, they would come down from the side of a mountain and merge with a hundred other cars on an L.A. freeway heading for home. He would text me a picture from his 7th floor sublet, with just three words: *This is amazing.*

As I stepped from my car on Tuesday morning, with the events of my son's journey still in the future, I looked to the north. The eyes of the homeless watched me. I averted my own, and slipped into the building, hoping with every inch of my being that they did not, for one moment, think that I had been mocking them.

Mugwumpishly tendered,


Corinne Corley

# Saturday Musings, 18 June 2011

Good morning,

The song of the mourning dove rises over the rooftops of the houses around me. The distant drone of cars on the main thoroughfare occasionally punctuates the stillness, along with the chatter of squirrels and an intermittent *whoop* of something I don't recognize. Morning; Brookside; another weekend.

I feel tension flowing from my body and breathe in fresh air to replace it. I am surrounded by a green veil of early summer leaves. I am hidden from traffic by the fluttering flag, the pale concrete of my porch, and a jumble of rocking chairs. My feet rest on an old grey rug, damp from the storm that briefly raged in the night. As creatures call to one another and a train cries in the distance, I am silent.

Over the gentle din of morning sounds, I hear another voice, speaking my name. I turn, and see a profile gone fourteen years this week. A strong chin, pale blue eyes, wide shoulders; a body in constant motion. I feel something long suppressed rise within me.

*Another day, another house, another morning.*

His figure huddled over a percolator. I stood a few feet away, observing surprisingly dense stubble on his chin and a sweep of straight black hair falling over his eyes. He glanced in my direction and muttered, *You don't look much better!* before turning back, waiting for the bubbling coffee to settle in its pot. When the noise of the brewing ceased, he filled two mugs, and handed one to me. I moved ahead of him, through the living room, and out onto my mother's porch.

We both were docked in our family home, my brother Steve and I. It was the fall of 1977, and I had just come home with my tail between my legs, from a ten-month attempt to establish myself in Boston. I had escaped there after a pale conclusion to an undistinguished college career marked by nothing more or less glamorous than a stumble across the commencement stage and a few dim memories of classes that I frequently skipped. If I was 22, my baby brother Stephen must have been not yet 18, and maybe still in high school.

We sat in metal lawn chairs, on the wide brick porch, gazing on the street where we had played as children. Neither of us spoke. My hangover gnawed at my stomach. I glanced over at my brother, nervous, wondering if he could tell. The silence lengthened.

After a few uneasy moments had passed, Steve turned towards me, earnest eyes searching my face. *What are you going to do now,* he asked.

I knew he didn't mean, now that I had awakened, feeling sick, and had doused my nausea with the thick black brew. I set my mug beside his and looked across the street. I studied the house where old lady Venable had lived and, I understood, where she had died. I remembered her standing at the fence of her backyard watching my brothers and their friends party, in 1970, when I was fifteen and my parents had taken their first vacation, leaving my sister Joyce in charge of us. We thought Mrs. Venable disapproved of the hippies, and the motorcycles, and the blare of the Grateful Dead from the stereo. We derided her, even as we feared that she would come across the street and tell our parents about our parties.

I sighed. *What was I going to do, now?* I had gone to Boston ostensibly to start graduate school at Boston College, but fell of my own negligible weight, stumbling over the nightlife of the actresses whose apartment I shared. They thrived in their day jobs and caroused with their friends, while I sat at the table and wished that I could have their lives. I fled when we learned that our building would be converted to co-ops, and they said they did not want me to move into their new digs. We advertised for a roommate, not a sister, one of them snapped at me. I packed my clothes, my books, and an old rocker that I found at a junk store in Cambridge, into the back of my brother Kevin's car, and retreated. That had been a month ago, and I had spent the intervening time getting reacquainted with my old haunts in the Central West End and pretending to look for work.

The morning waned around us, and the sounds of the neighborhood rose. I could hear my mother in the living room. She opened the drapes, and gave a little wave to her children. I spared her a thin smile and turned back to my brother. *I don't really know,* I finally admitted. *I can still go to grad school. SLU will still take me, in January.*

He studied me for a few minutes while I avoided his gaze. Then he looked away, into the yellow leaves of autumn that swayed in the morning breeze. *You ever wonder what the point is?* he finally asked.

I could have answered honestly. I could have told him that I would have done anything to avoid that question, and often did. I could have told him that I had not one inkling of what the point was, nor of how to begin to figure it out, and the drive to know took me behind the wheel of a car with Scotch in my veins and an iron vise gripping my stomach. I could have assured him that the point had thus far escaped me, and that the quest for it haunted me and lurked in every bad line of poetry I ever wrote.

Instead, I laughed. *No, not really, I told him. I'm not even sure there is a point.*

He stood, then. He tossed cold coffee into the yard, and gave out a quiet, pale chuckle. *Me neither,* he agreed. And the world turned a click to the right, as my mother opened the front door and summoned us to breakfast.

It's June, it's 2011, and I feel the warmth of the summer sun on my bare shoulders. I am hungry. The cursor dances on the screen, beneath the pale smears of dirt that I have let accumulate. Far away, in a small brass box adorned with a skull and roses sticker, the ashes of my brother Stephen have faded into a nearly painless memory.

Mugwumpishly tendered,


Corinne Corley

# Monday, June 25, 2012

*The Past Revisited: From August 2009*
*On Mon, Aug 24, 2009 at 6:16 AM, Corinne Corley wrote:*

Good morning,

It is still pitch black, too dark to venture onto my porch, so I am writing this from the breakfast nook of my airplane bungalow in Brookside.

For those of you who have not visited Kansas City or who are otherwise unfamiliar with the Craftsman Airplane Bungalow, this is a style of house that has its porch on the side, making the house resemble a one-winged airplane. In all of the houses in my neighborhood, the living room and dining room form an "L" shape, and there is a small nook, usually with original built-ins, between the dining room and the kitchen.

When I bought this house, the nook contained a white formica-top table, custom-built by the previous owner's father. Four sturdy white ladder-back chairs surrounded it, and at that table, my son ate most of his meals until 1997, when a small bequest from his uncle Stephen allowed us to get our first computer. Thereafter, meals were taken in the dining room, and the nook became Corinne's grotto.

You could not call this a room, although we often refer to it as my "office", in the Les Nessman sense of a private space that no one can invade without permission. I keep my angel collection on a shelf on the west wall, and to the east is a two-tiered wooden cabinet containing some Limoges and Haviland pieces that I inherited from my mother, including the seven-inch salad plate that my brother Mark and I purchased for eight dollars and gave her for Mother's Day forty years ago. My writing desk and an oak printer stand are crammed against the northwall, where the window opens onto the neighbor's rose trellis.

On the wall to the left of the window in front of me is a picture of my son at age 8, beneath which is a picture of a radiant Uncle Steve taken years ago, when we were all too young to know what the future held. To the right of the window is a small plaque that Patrick made, which reads, "Many hands make light work." Beneath this wise observation is a picture of my son at age 6, framed with a poem written in his hand, constructed from his the letters of his name, which reads: "Patient, Adventurous, Talented, Remarkable, Intelligent, Casual, Kind."

Patrick.

You knew I'd get there, didn't you -- how could I not?

But let me tell you something else first. Let me tell you about a cartoon called "Ed, Edd and Eddie," which is the story of three boys who are constant companions in one wild adventure after another. My son and I used to watch this cartoon together. In one episode, Ed is going to move out of the neighborhood and Edd laments the impending departure, wailing: *Who will push me on the swings? Who will butter my toast?* We found this line amusing, mimicking it whenever one of us left for the store, or work, or to go to the movies. *Who will butter my toast,* we had only to say, and peals of giggles or laughter would follow.

Patrick left for college this weekend. Penny Thieme and I drove him to Greencastle, Indiana. It is only fitting that Penny should be the one who accompanied us, since his summer and winter breaks during elementary school were spent with Aunt Penny and Uncle Ben. The two of them are golden threads shot through the tapestry of his life, and hers weaves long and strong through the patterns emerging from each motion of the shuttle. All of his aunts, by birth and by choice, have had special places in Patrick's formation, but Aunt Penny in particular imparted many lessons to Patrick that mothers just cannot convey. They share art, and they share memories of late-night movies, and they have an ease of being that I quite frankly envy. And she is calm and accepting, a perfect foil for my fussy personality. I knew I would need her strength on this trip.

The mound of stuff that we jammed into the Saturn astounded me. A refrigerator, a microwave, a cofee pot, a suitcase, three jam-packed duffle bags, an amp, two guitars, the pedal for the electric guitar, $150.00 worth of food from Costco, a butterfly chair, bedding, towels, a lamp, a waste-basket, and every drug store item that Katrina or I imagined he might need. I cleverly packed all the little things inside of containers that could serve duo purposes in a dorm room, and with Patrick and Penny, I leveraged each item into a nook, cranny or air pocket.

Only a few things got left behind, most of which were replaced in Greencastle. The electric guitar stand, I discovered on the hearth on my return last evening, and it will get shipped, along with his Dali posters, in the first care package.

The trip from Kansas City to St. Louis was uneventful. We found the Iron Barley without incident, and enjoyed an hour or so with my sister Joyce and her daughter Lisa. By seven Friday evening, we had arrived at the Holiday Inn in Cloverdale, where the three of us, hyped to the gills with road buzz, ate bananas, reminisced about Patrick's childhood, and talked of college until much later than we should have.

The system for off-loading freshman belongings is pretty remarkable at DePauw University. The parent is instructed to pull up as close to the student's dorm as possible, and to then deposit all of the student's possessions onto the sidewalk. The student -- or an auxiliary family member -- stations himself by the pile while you park the car, and then you commence sequential trips with armloads of boxes, bundles and baggage to and from your allocated square of cement. In that way, everything you've gathered to make the next nine months as comfortable as the first nine, gets transferred from sidewalk to room with an efficiency that amazed me.

In case you haven't seen a dorm room at DePauw University -- or anywhere else -- a single is 7 feet, 5 inches by 11 feet, 4 inches. It is a cement-block cube which contains a super-long twin bed, a plain desk with obligatory hutch, a bookshelf and a dresser, all made of solid, very heavy wood. As arranged by the housing staff, the dresser flanks one wall, across from which are the desk with its chair and two-shelf hutch, next to the dresser topped by the bookshelf. There are 18 inches of floor space between the two ordered rows of furniture spanning the length of the room.

While Patrick and I engaged in some parent-and-entering-freshman task, Penny decided that a different arrangement would be more commodious, as a consequence of which, the desk, bed and dresser formed a "C" and allowed for three square feet of moving room. With that framework, we were able to unpack everything, including shoving the bookshelf into the closet to serve as shelves for all that food, while stacking the fridge and microwave on the dresser. A corner was co-opted for the folding canvas chair; and the six inches between the bed and the dresser held the amp.

With everything unpacked, hung up, stashed and stored, we left the room to go to the convocation. As he locked the door of his room for the first time, I remarked to Patrick, *It's like you have your own apartment.* Came the rapid reply: *Yes, a really really tiny one.* As I laughed, he asked, *Do you know how many square feet the room is?* I had to confess that yes, I did -- *about 77-1/2. Yeah,* he sighed. *But at least my amp fit.*

We all have our priorities. I had felt the same way about the Costco goods -- my boy can surely survive the first month, I kept telling myself. Club crackers and peanut butter.

The students separated from their parents for the convocation. Penny and I drifted casually down to the performing arts center. A large volunteer, the first nominally unfriendly one I saw, tried to prevent me from entering the auditorium. *You can go to the balcony,* she said. I looked at the two steep flights of open metal stairs. *Impossible.* She then gestured to a side room. *Then go over to Moore Annex, and you can view it on video.*

Video? Watch the convocation on video? They had to be joking.

Of course, I did not yet know what a "convocation" was. Had I been quick, I might have explored the Internet to learn the meaning of this word. However, I knew from the weekend activity guide that the school president would be speaking, so I assumed it was an important event. This, I would not watch on video.

I am not ashamed to say that I played the ADA card, and got a seat on the main floor.

There we were ushered, Aunt Penny and I, into the midst of parents who had arrived early enough to get a seat in the best section without being pushy. Luckily, several chairs were still empty in the middle of the second row beyond the bank of seats reserved for the students, and into these the chastened volunteer led us. As we waited, the lights dimmed, and a huge screen dropped from the ceiling. A video began to play, depicting various members of the academic community talking about DePauw in reverent tones, or with animated voices, or with quiet confidence. I found their enthusiasm intriguing, and began to suspect that Patrick had chosen a very good place indeed.

And then the screen went blank. A hush descended over the assembly.

Seconds later, live feed commenced. I didn't understand what I was seeing, at first. But the parents around me began murmuring, and the sound of applause swelled. I squinted, furrowed my brow, peered intently at the images before me and suddenly, I realized what was happening -- and my friends, I began to cry.

The entire faculty of DePauw University had formed two lines in the long hallway outside of the auditorium in which I sat. The doors to the Center stood opened. Through those doors, one by one, in slow single file, came the Class of 2013, and as they processed into the building, they were given a standing ovation by their professors.

As the eight-hundred members of my son's class entered the auditorium, the waiting families began to clap as well. The acclamation resonated through the high-ceilinged room; the thunderous praise rang from the seats of parents, grandparents, guardians, siblings, uncles and aunts in the lower rows, rising to meet the roar from the balcony. My hands ached from clapping and still the students came, and still the faculty applauded, and still I cried, until each freshman had entered. Then the faculty entered and the students returned the ovation as the stage filled with professors, deans, and assistants, and even the student body president. The applause continued until each and every one of them reached their designated place, and then, in one grand moment, everyone sat -- and the hall was silent.

Speeches followed, some of which were tender and poignant. Poetry was read; advice dispensed; greetings spoken. In due course, we exited the hall and our children continued with freshman activities while we shoved soggy handkerchiefs into our pockets and marveled among ourselves that DePauw surely knows how to do things right.

At the appointed hour, we returned to the smallest apartment on the planet, for the hour designated on the written agenda to Say Goodbye to Families. The last few items had been purchased at CVS in a mad dash, and promises had been extracted -- take your medicine, wear your glasses, listen to your mentor, study hard, take good care of yourself. I walked out of his dorm room, followed by his beloved Penny.

I would not have heard him if the suite had not been empty, but it was. And so, I did hear him when he said, in the very quietest of little-boy-whispers, from inside his allocated seventy-seven square feet,

*"Who will push me on the swings. . . who will butter my toast?"*

We laughed, then, my nearly-six-feet tall son and I; and he let me hug him, and we all went down to the car. A few last things were shoved into his hands -- more cash; the paper from the freshmen service project; a copy of the housing contract. We scrambled to find his glasses; Penny teased him about girls; and, too quickly, with a casual flick of his hand, he turned, and walked back into Hogate Hall. I was left standing on the sidewalk where once his pile of stuff had been, wondering what on earth I was thinking, leaving my only child in a strange place eight hours from home, with nothing more to protect him than his inherited charm and unlimited Verizon Wireless texting.

In my heart of hearts, I know my fears are unfounded. He will suffer no more indignities than any young man starting college; and he will have as many glorious moments of stunning self-discovery. He will come home taller, more self-confident, and with a new hair cut that some cute freshman girl decides to make him to get. There will eventually come a holiday that he does not spend with me; and then he will do a winter term abroad; and, eventually, I will turn his bedroom into a sewing room, or a library, or a storage space for broken suitcases.

The weaver chooses her patterns, and the threads from which her work will be constructed. Not so the parent. We are more akin to the sculptor -- or perhaps the puppeteer. Like Giuseppe, I wanted a real boy, and that is precisely what I got. He has come to life now -- and I would not stop his dancing if I could.

Mugwumpishly tendered,


Corinne Corley

# Saturday Musings, 25 June 2011

Good morning,

I don't know how I came to be this old, middle-aged woman living in a small, comfortable house in Kansas City. It seems mere moments ago that it is December of 1976, when I left Missouri to start a life in Boston.

I feel again the lift of the planet from the runway at Lambert, and once again my stomach falls as the jet pitches and rolls in the winter sky. I am 21, and skinny, and I have just cut off three feet of hair and painted blond streaks in the resultant back-combed waves.

At the other end, at Logan, I am met by a friend, David Sotkowitz, who throws my suitcase in the back of his car in the snowy drifts of the short-term parking lot. The snap of cold air bites my cheeks, and I shudder in a coat that would have been more than adequate for Missouri winter but does nothing in Boston's December. We chatter, exchanging accounts of events since we last saw one another in a St. Louis summer, as he completed graduate school and I got ready to enter my last semester of college.

An hour later, after midnight, I lie on a makeshift pallet in a spare corner of his apartment, watching a new, vigorous snowfall. The ground outside holds seventeen inches, and another eleven inches will fall in the night, a heavy, silent shroud. I stand at the window in the morning, holding a cup of tea, wondering if I should grab my suitcase and go back to the Midwest. *I am not this brave*, I tell myself.

After a few days, I venture to the Boston College student life office, and page through a notebook of roommate listings. I use their phone to make a few appointments, then take the trolley downtown to meet my new boss at the job arranged for me by my most recent St. Louis employer. As the trolley slips underground, and the dark surrounds me in that brief moment before the lights come up, I feel the warm flush of fear. *What do I think I am doing*, I ask myself. I cannot answer.

In time, I learned to navigate the green line with ease. I never lost the slight surge of panic when the car traversed from trolley to subway, or the anxiousness of waiting in an underground station after the sun had set. But I developed some moderate adeptness, a passable ability to cling to an overhead bar so that an old lady could have my seat. I could, after a few weeks, read in a standing position. Though not a native, I could pass.

One evening, tired from work, I leaned against a pillar awaiting the train for home. My eyes drifted closed, and I felt my body sag. The low murmur of evening riders surrounded me. The cavernous underground stations hummed with the thunder of distant cars rambling through tunnels, barreling through the gloom of the spider web of which the Massachusetts Transit system is comprised.

I felt a gentle pull on the strap of my handbag. My eyes flew open and I grabbed my purse, stepping swiftly away from the body at my shoulder. I moved backwards, clutching my belongings against my chest, scrambling away from the groping hand.

I met his eyes. Dark orbs in sunken hollows, over crusty grime, surrounded by greasy, uncut hair. Raw, red lips; reaching hands with ragged fingerless gloves. The mouth gaped and sounds emitted, croaks that I recognized as words but could not distinguish. We stood, the thief and I, our gazes caught in an unending grip.

And then the train pulled into the station, with squealing brakes, and the rush of automatic doors. I tore my eyes away from the pathetic sight of my attacker, and stepped backwards, into a waiting car. I stood in the gap as commuters shoved past me, falling into seats. I remained at the entryway, watching the man, until the doors closed, and the train lurched forward. Darkness embraced me. I moved towards a bench, and lowered myself to sit, as the weary passengers adjusted to accommodate my small frame.

A storm has gathered as I sat on my porch, here in the Midwest, in the cool of early summer. Thunder rumbles in the distant air. I am hungry, and I have chores to do. Although I have not miles to go before I sleep, still, my day is full, and there will be little time for sitting around, lost in idle dreams about the past.

Mugwumpishly tendered,


Corinne Corley

# Saturday Musings, 02 July 2011

Good morning,

Yesterday afternoon, my son and I sat without talking through the long crescendo of *The Tree of Life*. In the soft darkness of the old movie theatre, I felt a flood of memories overwhelm me -- the twitch of fear at the raised voices of my childhood; unbearable love engulfing me while I huddled in my mother's determined embrace; later, stark shock as I clutched a telephone receiver to my ear and asked, *which brother?* The movie's narrative followed strikingly familiar contours, mirroring in many ways the tumbled path of my life -- uncanny, unreal, unrelenting and astonishing.

I am transported back in time by one scene of the movie in particular, in which the family celebrated the 4th of July. I feel again a small line of sweat trickle between my narrow shoulder blades, in the heat of an Independence Day decades ago, long forgotten. I see the shadowy angles of my brothers' faces, as they wave sparkler after dazzling sparkler high above their heads to slice through the summer night. I press against the brick wall on my mother's porch, far away from the blazing flare that my father has jammed into the ground. Its crimson flames shoot straight into the inky sky. A rush of terror floods through me; delicious, delirious. I grip my brother's arm. Firecrackers burst, brief and furious.

Hours later, I lie in the bottom bunk bed in the room that I share with one of my sisters and listen to my parents arguing. My siblings sleep. Alone, I huddle under a thin cover in the stifling heat. The air stirs only when the oscillating fan spans in my direction.

My father's voice rises as my mother's tone descends. I cannot breathe. I wrap my arms around my chest, and squeeze my eyes more tightly closed. I will them to stop the dance that never ends. I bargain with God. I doubt that anyone hears my promises, but still I make them: *Don't let him hit her,* I pray, *and I promise I will be good for the rest of my life.* I fall asleep, still holding myself close, still murmuring my endless litany of shame.

In the morning our yard is strewn with the litter of our festivities. I rise before anyone else, before my mother, before my father, before my seven brothers and sisters. I slip into a pair of sandals and go outside in my pajamas. I gather the trash and dump the bucket of water down the driveway. I stuff discarded wrappers, spent whirligigs, and the rubble of flares and sparklers into a brown paper bag, and cram that into the steel trash can. I sweep away the ashes of snakes that my brothers lit at the top of the cement stairs in our front yard. By the time my mother shuffles into the kitchen to start the percolator, I am back in the house, sitting on the sofa, reading.

She greets me in her most quiet voice, the one that she uses when she does not want to disturb my father. I answer her in kind, and she lowers her body to rest beside me. *Happy 5th of July,* she tells me, and I snuggle against her frail form. I couldn't sleep last night, I admit to her, and I feel the tension in her response. *It's okay,* she assures me. *Everything is okay.*

I believe her because I want her to be right. As the smell of coffee rises around us, I bury my nose in my book, and she lights a cigarette. Our whispered pact binds us together; our lies keep us chained to our place.

Mugwumpishly tendered,


Corinne Corley

# Saturday Musings, 03 July 2010

Good morning,

I turned the alarm off before sleeping last night, but I could not extinguish the internal bells, and so I awakened, as usual, just before six. As I stretched before rising, each muscle protested the brutal week's legacy of tension. My neck has stiffened; the diagonal nerve running under my left shoulder tingles, nagging me, announcing the onset of a shingles outbreak. I am weary.

Last night, I rested, for a few sweet, brief moments, on a bench in English Landing Park, on the banks of the Missouri River, as the sun sank, and the children played, and the swift, sure current pushed its sweep of backwater under the bridge to my left. With my companion's arm across my shoulders, I watched a fisherman cast his line over and over, in a wide, sweeping arc.

Walkers quietly passed on the trail behind us, some pushing strollers, others holding leashes from which eager dogs bounded. The heat of the day dissipated. A cool breeze caressed my face. I closed my eyes, and the river in front of me could have been any river, any where, at any time of my life.

I have always been fond of water. When I was 8 or 9, my mother discovered an unused beach near the Alton Dam in

Illinois. Thus began a perfect year of impromptu outings after she finished her shift at Famous-Barr. She preferred to picnic in early spring and late autumn, when nobody else in their right mind would think to swim, or throw a blanket down to partake of wax paper-wrapped peanut-butter and jelly sand-wiches and jars of cold, home-made lemonade.

There is an official park near the Dam these days, but in my childhood, the area we preferred was just a stretch of grass with no designated purpose, abutting a stand of scraggy trees and spanning a long undeveloped stretch of water. Alton sits at the confluence of three rivers -- the Missouri, the Missis-sippi, and the Illinois. I close my eyes and picture the dam to my right, over a small hill, rising with its rusted, frightening edifice that my brother Mark dared me to scale as my mother smoked Kents and lazily scolded him in tones so casual that no one took her seriously. I see the river in front of me; and I cannot say which river, or where in the confluence configura-tion this little haven sat.

I don't know how my mother found the place. I can't remember how old I was, or whether my little brothers ac-companied us. But I remember putting on my old Keds and walking across the packed, wet sand into the river, wearing a faded one-piece swimming suit, my hair tied in braids around my head.

Mother required us to swim wearing our shoes. My brothers protested, but I obeyed without question. I believed her stories of other, less loved children with their bleeding, unshod feet, stepping on debris, or being nipped by small, blind creatures that lived deep in the murky water.

We rarely encountered other picnickers during that first year. We went weekly, through the hot days of summer and into the cool of the fall. We had our last outing there in late October. We could not swim; we wore jackets, slacks, socks and heavy shoes. The thermos held hot cocoa. My mother sat wrapped in a sweater, in an aluminum lawn chair with green webbing. She smiled and smoked, as we dragged sticks across the sidewalk and wrote our names in crooked letters that extended the length of the sodden sand next to the overgrown grass.

During that school year, the Post-Dispatch ran an article about the Dam, and my mother fretted over the story. *There goes our picnic spot,* she complained. And she was right: When we went there for the first time in the spring, several families had arrived ahead of us, and they had already claimed the lone wooden table.

We took to making our picnics during the week, hoping to avoid the growing Saturday crowd. My mother disdained the commonplace and the popular -- she preferred to forge new paths rather than follow those worn by the trodding of others. I did not understand her moods at the time, though I think I do now, with the clear, unfettered vision of hindsight. At the time, we only knew that we loved those picnics; we loved the cold bite of the river when we first waded into it, and the sweet ooze of jelly as we bit into our sandwiches. We did not want to sacrifice the wicked thrill of climbing up the side of the dam and staring into the docks, or the exhilaration of running too far along the riverbanks, while my mother called warnings after us -- warnings that even she knew we would ignore.

A sense of urgency settled on my brothers and me. We knew that our visits to the dam would occur with increasing infrequency until eventually, we would stop going altogether and my mother would find some other place for our picnics. Our tones became desperate, relentless, as we wheedled and pleaded.

*Can we go to the beach? Can we? Oh come on Mom -- it won't be crowded! Come on! It's early! Nobody but us goes on picnics at seven in the morning, Mom!*

On an especially hot Saturday, we started begging before breakfast. We nagged our mother until she capitulated and agreed to take us despite her misgivings. The air of the day hung in humid sheaths around us as we clamored out of the car in the expanse of gravel south of the beach. We snatched the canvas bag of towels and the picnic basket, barely stopping to close the car doors as we ran towards the picnic area. The sight around the corner brought us to a staggering halt.

A group of thirty or forty children, about our age, with a small clutch of grown-ups, swarmed the shrinking stretch of sand flanking the river. Mark, Kevin and I stood, a mixture of awe and horror spread across our faces. The children in front of us streamed towards the river, boys in cut-off shorts, girls wearing mostly just underwear and T-shirts, having discarded their britches in piles next to the folding chairs on which their mothers and fathers lounged in the heavy heat of the late morning air.

My mother struggled to remain cheerful as we found a small spot on which to spread our blanket. Silently, with some reluctance, and worried glances -- backward, to our mother, outwards, to the noisy group -- my brothers and I got ready for a swim. Mother settled into her chair and poured a glass of lemonade. We took this as her unspoken permission to enjoy ourselves, and ran towards the water.

I don't know which one of us heard the children's wails first. We had been swimming for long enough to wrinkle our skin; I remember standing on the beach, gazing without comprehension at the disturbance near the bend around which the river met the dam. I looked down at my hands, seeing the flesh of my fingers bunched in tight, white whorls.

My brothers pulled me towards children huddled on the side of the river as our mother ran up behind us, calling our names, bidding us to *stop, stop, stop*. I cannot help but recall that all of the other people at the beach that day were black. Their color had no importance to me at the time but it haunts me now. I remember how dark they were, how different from me. I do not know from where they came; whether they came from the City; or even, who they were. I had been raised without prejudice, so I had not noticed this at first.

And in truth, their skin color has no significance to me other than this: I remember their eyes: stark brown against bold white, as they watched a man carrying the small, still body of a little girl from the silent river. I remember the color of her skin -- a horrid, dull grey, without the rush of her blood, the beat of her heart, the draw of air through her small lungs. And I remember the bright red plastic clips in the many, sodden braids on her tiny, delicate head, which fell, lifeless, against her father's heaving chest.

I have found solace near the river. I have slept, in my own home, in the still of the mountains, with a river rushing past at its height, in the shank of an Ozark spring. I have waded in cold water on smooth flagstone, and I have set myself down and let the water comfort me. But I have not forgotten that the river once claimed the life of a little black girl, in Alton, in my childhood, while my mother smoked and worried about things of which I had no real understanding, and my brothers and I fretted over the loss of our special, private place.

Mugwumpishly tendered,


Corinne Corley

# Saturday Musings, 07 July 2012

Good morning,

The heat has broken, at least for one sweet morning, though the potted plants on my deck have shriveled despite the constant watering and desperate deployment of a spray bottle. A few petunias gamely struggle; the begonias sighed and died; the Gerber daisies have shriveled; one of the two bright pink plants, the names of which I no longer recall, turned to dusty shreds. The other has blackened buds, hard and sad, that foretell its pending demise. *I should have brought the plants into the house when the heat wave struck*, I tell myself; now it is too late.

In times past, when the children whose high, happy voices gave vibrant life to this home cavorted in the driveway, we dragged a large pool to the backyard, stood it in the middle of a twelve-foot wide sand pile, and created our own beach. A Little Tykes slide angled over the side of the pool into the shimmering water. In a box, in the attic maybe -- or on a high shelf in the basement -- pictures of those summers rest against old letters, fading drawings made from Cray Pas, and gilded, ribbonned, letters of commendation.

As I conspired with him the other day to orchestrate a repair to a much-cherished guitar belonging to my son, my friend Alan paused and raised his hand. *Do you remember this,* he said, palm turned towards me, keeping me still, while

Alan summoned the memory. *Do you remember when you said: "A boy? What on earth am I going to do with a boy?"*

I remember.

I lay in a gigantic heap, on a gurney, in a sterile room in Little Rock, at the University of Arkansas' genetic testing laboratory. A technician sat on a low stool between me and a monitor, with an ultra sound wand in one gloved hand, the head of the wand pressed against my belly. *Do you want to know the gender,* she asked. *No, I don't, I replied. It's a boy! she crowed,* unable to contain herself.

*A boy? A boy? What on earth am I going to do with a boy?*

I have my answer now.

With that boy, I learned so many life's lessons that they fill my heart and spill out into the world around me.

That boy announced, in a baby's voice, that he would be the one to get the newspaper from our apartment door-step, the first winter we moved back to Kansas City. He could barely reach the knob of our front door, but turn it he did. He bent down to get the Kansas City Star for me, the January before he turned two, and each day thereafter until we moved in May. *Your legs don't work so good, Mommy,* he told me. *Patrick get the paper for you.*

When I fell on the ice at the end of our driveway, in the home we bought that year, he toddled down the street to our neighbors' home down to get help. He was two and a half.

When I tripped over a gutter hiding under the snow in the dog run one dark night the next winter, that boy felt that I had been outside too long, and telephoned the same neighbor. All ten of my toes were broken. The neighbor found me lying, nearing numbness, at the side of the house on a bed of crystalline snow.

At five, that boy reached down into a hotel swimming pool to grab my shoulder as I sputtered and struggled, gasping for breath, my spastic legs unable to propel me from the deep end. He held me out of the water, patiently waiting for someone to come. A passing guest saw this stunning tableau through the large glass window that fronted on the lobby, and ran into the pool area. Through my coughing, as I sagged against the concrete, I heard the man say, *You did good, son, you did real good. Your Mom's going to be okay.*

With that boy, I climbed a mountain, conquered my fear of heights, and stood on the edge of a canyon to watch a cluster of birds swoop into the depths from which we had come.

Beside that boy, I journeyed deep into Carlsbad Cavern, beyond the accessible trail, raising my eyes to see the wondrous formations above me, slithering through narrow passages, my hand in his small one, his seven-year-old frame leading the way.

I traversed uneven ground, leaning on a walker, with a newly operated knee, to see that boy receive his Arrow of Light, which to this day nestles in a box on my dresser.

I walked the halls of the Mayo Clinic with that boy, and watched him pedal his bike around a lake in Rochester. I laughed when he asked if we could live in that hotel forever. With that boy, I sat in a small office to hear the verdict: The doctors in Kansas City were wrong. Your boy does not have Addison's disease.

A year later, I ignored that boy's determined refusal to board a plane to Mexico, despite the weeks of planning, the months of speaking Spanish by text message, the doctor's clearance to travel, the hours of filling out paperwork for the scholarship. I ignored his expressions of apprehension. I knew the time for him to fly had arrived.

Six weeks later, I barely recognized him as he followed other passengers into the waiting area, with his dark tan, his once-long hair now in short, thick curls around his head. *I was not just the tallest kid in the group,* he chuckled. *I was the tallest person in the whole country!* Later, after we dropped off the friend who had ridden to the airport with me, he softly admitted: *I am so glad you made me go!*

I quietly listened to that boy tell me a classmate had said that he was *too white to go to this school,* and I smiled, three years later, when that boy was elected president of his senior class. *There were five candidates,* he said, dismissively. *I just split the vote.* Still.

I slid into a ditch in a blizzard with that boy, en route to my cousin's funeral, our hearts racing. We looked at each other with something between terror and glee. With the white raging all around us, we crept up the exit ramp in our Chevy Blazer, slowly edging into the parking lot of a restaurant, where we ordered soup and waited out the storm.

That boy has walked me down two aisles, visited me in three hospitals, traveled to ten or twelve states with me, and invented characters and voices to make me laugh in times when my despair permeated the air.

I walked across urban Chicago campuses with that boy, assuring him that yes, he could manage far from home. I stood at the entry to a broad green campus, in Indiana, in March of 2009, and told him that we would find a way to make his attendance there happen.

I watched him struggle through that first year of college, and regroup, the summer after.

I watched him soar for the next two years, with friends, heartbreaks, good grades, and a crummy summer job from which he learned a valuable lesson. I have read the stories published under his name in his campus literary review, year after year. I've sat in a distant room, listening to the increasingly complex sounds of his guitar.

And a month ago, I packed that Chevy Blazer, and sent him off to Hollywood.

At 1:50 p.m., CDST, on Sunday, 08 July 2012, that boy will vanish. He will be 21 at that very moment. He will stand as he has always stood despite his many fears and trepidations: Smiling that slight, steady smile. Determined, strong, capable. And at long last, I will have my answer.

*What on earth am I going to do with a boy?*

Watch him grow to be a man.

Happy Birthday, Patrick Charles Corley. My pride in you is boundless.

Mugwumpishly tendered,


Corinne Corley

# Saturday Musings, 23 July 2011

Good morning,

The unbearable heat of summer lurks an hour from where I now sit, in a blond-wood rocker, on my porch, with my five-dollar estate sale table as a laptop perch. Beside me, the old porch chair abandoned by a departing law school friend sits with only an exercise ball for company. Its joints gave way a few weeks ago and have not yet been re-glued. The plants on their stands seem happier for several days of excessive watering. The occasional neighbor listlessly wanders down the cracked sidewalk, getting in a few feet of exercise before the temperature rises. The gas man pulls into the driveway behind my Saturn, and the morning's activity begins.

But I have drifted into the past, as I tend to do on these lazy days. My surroundings fade, and in their place appears a wooden porch in Winslow, Arkansas, built by a carpenter friend with lines that come to an apex in the middle of the highway. I appreciated the artistry, although natives often stood and wondered at the foolishness. *Middle of the road,* they mused, shaking their heads at the oddness of it. *Huh, well, don't that beat all.*

Heat surrounded me that afternoon, the thick, cowardly southern heat that flees at sunset with the sweep of the mountain's evening chill. With a glass of cool well water on the table and a book in my hand, I daydreamed about the life I planned to lead in my new home.

A year later, I would have erected a wooden fence on the property line and would not have been visible from the highway. But that day, anyone passing could see me idling away a perfect Saturday, and sure enough, someone did. An old Chevy truck, from the late '50s or early '60s, pulled down my gravel drive. As it slowed, I squinted, trying to see the driver. In those parts, in those days, most anyone would stop for most any reason, but usually I would recognize a neighbor's face.

This one had nothing about it that seemed familiar. Creased lines on either side of a lean jaw, light brown stubble, home-shorn hair. I judged the man to be in his mid-30s. He stepped lightly across my yard, and stood below the spot where I had risen to greet him. *Mornin',* he ventured. I returned the comment, glancing over at his vehicle.

I could see a woman in the passenger seat, and a couple of kids peering around the rusty side of the truck. Small children, none too clean, and hungry-looking. I turned my attention back to their father.

The slimness of his face topped an even thinner body, but his arms looked strong and his shoulders square. I knew what would come next. He had not stopped to beg, but to ask about work, and I started thinking about what I could have him do that might allow me to give him a few dollars with which to feed his family. The '80s had been hard on country folk, with dogged droughts and a collapse of the free-wheeling economy of the '70s. These wanderers might otherwise have been working a farm that had been in their family for generations.

I did not have to wait long for the man's request. In a voice that did not tell of the pain it caused him to inquire, he asked if I had any chores that he might do. I thought about the rick of wood that could be re-stacked, the north plot of land that needed bush-whacking, a door frame that sagged in the unfinished addition. I nodded, and gestured for the family to disembark from the truck's dusty confines.

The woman showed herself to be in her late 20's, with a boy eight and a girl six. The children ran around the front yard while their mother and I made lemonade, and their father dragged my small tool collection out to get done what he could before the sun set. I found myself chattering to the kids with their silent mother alongside me, and my nephew's calico cat, George, whom I had inherited when my nephew developed asthma, running around with the boy chasing her.

I fed them grilled cheese sandwiches with thin slices of tomatoes purchased from a farm up the road. The man ate his while standing alongside the porch but the woman refused what I offered. The boy ate two and the girl one and a half, and when I had washed the few dishes, I came back outside to find the mother sweeping the floorboards of my new porch, while the children napped on the seat of the truck, and the man cleaned the blades of my mower.

I gave the man some money, more than the hours he worked might be considered worth, and silently watched as his wife calculated whether they would find somewhere to sleep on the strength of it. I put a bag of cookies into the woman's hands, the set of my mouth telling her not to protest. The man gently hustled his children into the bed of the vehicle, helping his wife into the cab, softly closing the door for her. I looked beyond the little scene, to the curve of the hill on the east side of the highway, and the line of trees that followed the mountainside to the neighboring farms. Those trees would sway with the mildest of winds, but they stood motionless in the heat of the late afternoon.

With his family secured, the man had only to turn and thank me. I folded my arms across my chest, and fastened a smile on my face. By thirty-four years of age, I had suffered my share of humiliation, and did not lightly visit any on another human being. I would make his task painless if I could. *Thank you kindly for what you did for me today,* I told him.

*You can't know what it's like, living out here on my own, being unable to do those chores.*

He paused. The brown of his eyes met the grey-blue of mine. We heard a jay call to its mate, in the still of the afternoon air. A long moment eased between us. He broke his gaze, then, and glanced at the land to the north of my house. *You oughtn't tell people you're alone,* he said then. *There's some might not have ought but bad on their minds.* I conceded his point with a little shrug. *Some mightn't,* I admitted. He nodded, just once. *Well, thanks for the food and such, ma'am,* he said, finally. I put out my hand, and the slim one he put into it felt strong and cool. He met my eyes again, and nodded again. *Might be, I'll be back this way, in a couple of weeks, and I'll check on you,* he said, and then, with a smooth maneuver that raised very little dust, he pulled his truck back out onto Highway 7, and headed north, into Fayetteville.

The gas man has finished replacing our meter, and the heat of the Kansas City summer has settled around me. I pull myself back into the present, and watch as the worker backs his truck onto Holmes Street, and drives away, to his next appointment.

Mugwumpishly tendered,


Corinne Corley

# Saturday Musings, 30 July 2011

Good morning,

A spray of rain greeted me at the back door today, and I made it welcome. It brought a rush of warm air into the kitchen, against which I finally had to close the door and retreat into my dining room with a cup of cooling coffee beside the sprawl of perused paper. Congress wrangles still; the President stands helpless; the partisan snarling resonates through the marble halls of our capitol. The world spins; the sun rises with its usual disdain for our shenanigans. As thunder ripples through the air, I note the ragged growth of vegetation in our side yard, raising unchecked fronds to the spray of water feeding its thirsty roots.

My week felt like a lumpy mattress. I negotiated a last-minute settlement in a troubling case, in which my client gave more than he needed to sacrifice -- once again, and for the good of his children. He did so with clear-headed reasoning, driven by his hope, as always, that his children would have a better life because he put their needs before his own. His hope echoes my prayer.

I sat beside my mother-in-law at dinner this week, listening to her sweetly narrated story of her and her twin sister playing their respective pianos from distant rooms in their childhood home. Her eighty-year-old frailty touched my heart, and put me in mind of another twin, just as old, just as frail, whom I met a couple of light years ago.

Her name was Evalyn, and her twin had died long before I met her back in my prosecutor days. Because justice is never swiftly dealt, we had decided to record her testimony to insure that we would be able to use her words and have the jury see the shuddering, sweet vulnerability of her somewhat vacant smile.

A video camera turned its objective eye in her direction from the far corner of the room. The defendant whom we had accused of stealing Evalyn's money did not attend; she huddled, instead, in a jail cell, her bond deliberately set at a level that we hoped would prevent her from finding another elderly victim while we awaited the trial date. The public defender sat at one end of the table. Evalyn had eased her frail form onto the hard, unglamorous chair of a county conference room opposite him. My boss and I flanked her, I to the left, my boss to the right.

Evalyn had perceived the importance of the occasion, dressing as she might have to attend a church service. A stiffly ironed lace collar spanned the short space of her small neckline. The soft wool of a sweater surrounded her narrow shoulders, fastened in the center by a single pearl button. She folded her hands in her lap, holding a white handkerchief. When she had gotten settled, she turned toward the public defender, and graciously signaled him to proceed.

My boss stirred. Since this was a deposition to preserve testimony, scheduled at our behest, she went first. She asked the series of questions that would establish identity and ownership of the account on which we believed the defendant had cashed a series of unauthorized checks. The camera did not pause once during the proceedings; its minder stood impassively behind the tri-pod as Evalyn acknowledged, with a barely perceptible tinge of confusion, that she was indeed the only authorized signatory on the account. *My sister Edith used to share this account,* she told us. *But she's gone now.*

She stayed on task through the predicate facts of the case. No, the defendant did not have her permission to write checks on the account. No, she had no knowledge of the checks in question, at which she gazed for a few troubled moments before casting them with discernible disgust upon the table. We held our breaths, my boss and I, as she chuckled over a few random anecdotes about the defendant, who had somehow come to live in her guestroom, by some trickery the details of which I have never understood.

Finally, the basic facts established and the vulnerability of the victim recorded for future jurors to compare with mental images of their own grandmothers, my boss ended her questioning. The three of us turned toward the public defender, a young man who has since risen to higher offices, one of which he still holds. In those days, though, he was a slender, dark-headed earnest but inexperienced attorney, whom everyone nonetheless expected to treat our witness with tenderness and care.

He did not disappoint. In fact, his voice held so little force as to be almost inaudible, and I smothered a smile. He tried, without success, to establish senility on Evalyn's part, to suggest to future triers-of-fact that permission had been given and then forgotten. I did not blame him. I would have done the same in his place, though I could never have defended his client myself.

The woman in question had left other depleted bank accounts. One belonged to a man whom she relocated from St. Joseph to Kansas City in an effort to avoid an imminent prosecution. Her victim had died before his statement could be taken. I met with the police detective who had investigated, and he had no doubt that our defendant should have been made to pay for what she had done to the poor fellow. On the strength of some circumstantial evidence, including the defendant's description to paramedics of how the St. Joseph man had collapsed just before dying in his Plaza apartment, we had exhumed his body and had an autopsy done. But too much time had past, and the likely agent of his death, arsenic, could not have survived the formaldehyde with which his body had been filled.

Still, I did not doubt that she had hastened his death. I stood in the cold, clean room in which the coroner performed the examination of his pristine, preserved body, my gaze fixed on a spattering of mold on the prayer book in his hands, and the Rosary entwined around them. I watched without flinching, without gagging, so intent was I on prosecuting this woman for his death. The police officers assigned to record the event snapped photo after photo, until red spots drifted before my eyes, but still I stood, a willing witness to desecration in the name of justice.

Afterwards, I burned the dress I had worn, the same dress I had worn the prior year to my mother's funeral. I could not get the smell of decay out of its fabric.

But Evalyn had not been killed, and she sat between the two of us, her protectors, waiting for the next question. The defendant's counsel seemed to hesitate, and, finally, he violated the cardinal rule of questioning: He asked something to which he did not already know the answer. *How could my client have gotten your signature so perfect,* he inquired.

Evalyn's eyes sparkled. No one in the room doubted the intelligence with which she had navigated the world, as she lifted her slender, quivering hand to raise the proferred exhibit, a copy of one of the forged checks. She held it out, a few inches higher than her face, and turned her mischievous eyes toward the public defender. *The same way me and Edith made our mother's signature, on our report cards,* she told him. *We snuck into her desk and got a letter that she had written. We put the report card from our teacher against a window, the letter behind it. And we traced our mother's signature onto it!* As she spoke, she moved a bony finger and traced her own signature, loop after loop, line after shaky line. And everyone in the room could see her long-dead twin beside her: two gleeful, clever girls in pigtails and pinafores, forging their mother's name to a card full of bad marks.

The camera recorded the whole thing.

As I sat beside my mother-in-law this week, watching her sweet smile, listening as she remembered the way she and her twin did everything together, through childhood, through college, and in the early years of their married lives, I thought about Evalyn. She has surely died by now. She must be somewhere pleasant, sitting beside her sister, cackling about the pranks they pulled, and the chagrin on their mother's face when they were found out. As for the woman who probably killed that poor old man, and certainly stole thousands of dollars from the old people on whom she preyed, I can only hope that she served out her time and found no further victims.

The brief thunderstorm has spent itself. My old Mac has just two minutes left on its battery, and duty calls. The other sentient beings in my household are either still sleeping, or have fallen back into a lazy dream, the Saturday sudoku lying on the floor, forgotten. Nearby, the dog snores in her bed, while the old girl cat watches from her chosen perch on the little bench in the hallway.

Mugwumpishly tendered,


Corinne Corley

132

# Saturday Musings, 06 August 2011

Good morning,

My neighbor has just tooled down our shared driveway, with a jaunty wave and a few minutes' conversation about a possible joint trip to the Planning Committee meeting in September. A stack of boards straddles her yard, delivered by Home Depot for her contractor husband to build a small deck on the side of our house, similar to one he built for them. Two boys stroll south on my street, their high voices drifting over to me, with the hint of daring of children everywhere, on the last true weekend of summer before area schools drop like dominoes into autumn.

The weekend hangs between a quiet week of intense work and a search for the perfect receptionist for my suite, and a scheduled trial in which two reasonably good parents will fight for principal residential custody of their thirteen-year-old triplet sons. Having raised one boy to age twenty, I think it likely that they each need some help from the other and I have put out overtures for some type of settlement, but I prepare for the worst while hoping that my feelers will take root in the remaining soil of the wasteland that their marriage has become.

In weeks like these, I wonder, time and time again, why I did not take the easy route. I could have, I suppose, married a neuro-surgeon, had 2.75 children, and lived in a swank suburban sprawling compound. I could have gone to lunch while my toddlers dabbled under the eyes of their nanny. Or I could have exited college into the waiting arms of the Peace Corps, and journeyed to points south, distant undeveloped lands where whatever skills I had as an unenlightened twenty-something might have been exploitable.

I have been asked, often, why I went to law school. I give various answers. My favorite quip involves having chosen law as a potential vocation in which I could write for a living. The truth is somewhat shabbier. I had been in graduate school, and my program lost its funding. The nine enrollees in the non-Masters-track Ph.D. program had received an invitation to finish our dissertations at another university, but at considerably higher and, for me, prohibitive cost. With student loans waiting to be paid if I halted my education, I did what I could do to delay repaying them: I applied to law school.

The state of Missouri, Department of Vocational Rehabilitation, kindly footed the bill. A friend from Kansas City, a Legal Aid Lawyer in the 70's who later graced the bench in Jackson County, encouraged me to investigate that potential. To do so, I made an appointment in the St. Louis City Voc Rehab office, which, if memory serves, occupied grungy space in an otherwise empty office building on Grand.

A receptionist showed me to the counselor's room. He sat behind a government issue putty-colored desk. He did not rise to greet me, which I found odd until he turned to take a binder from a shelf behind him, and I saw that he was sitting in a wheelchair.

*I'm Dick Goodwin,* he told me. *And I'm feeling kind of embarrassed,* I replied. He turned his head to one side, studying me quizzically. *Why is that?* he finally asked.

I gestured. Neither of us misunderstood my point. He drew a breath and nodded. *Oh, the chair,* he said, in a voice that meant, *you idiot woman, don't you think I know I'm in a wheelchair.* He pulled my application towards him, adjusted his glasses, and read in silence for a few minutes. *This says you have hereditary spastic paraplegia,* he noted, naming the now-debunked diagnosis under which I suffered for half of my life. It was my turn to dip my head, in my own acknowledgement of the statement of obvious fact.

We sat for a few minutes without speaking, Dick Goodwin and I. He scrawled a few lines on the bottom of the pages which I had completed. He made a stray mark on my doctor's report. He grabbed another binder, pulled a few more forms to the pile assembled before him, and noted a couple of things on one or two pages before looking back at me. *The state of Missouri considers you moderately to severely disabled, he told me. We'll pay your tuition at any state university that you care to attend to get a terminal degree that could lead to meaningful professional employment, and we'll give you a monthly stipend towards your living expenses.*

It came to nothing more or less than the approval of this man, whose life held more profound challenges than mine. I took his approval form, and exited the office, following his directions to the next phase, which consisted of a series of tests intended to identify fields in which I might be expected to attain some measure of success despite my moderate to severe disability.

Six months later, I started law school in Kansas City. I never saw Dick Goodwin again, but I had contact with him on a regular basis. In the fall of 1982, when I got a ticket for parking in the handicapped space in front of the law school despite my state-issued placard, despite my moderate to severe disability, I called upon him for back-up.

He wrote a letter to the Major in the University Police who had supported his ticket-issuing officer. Mr. Goodwin informed Major Garrett that the State of Missouri, Department of Vocational Rehabilitation, would be most happy to ask their attorneys to file a lawsuit against him, the University of Missouri at Kansas City, and anyone else who wrongfully interfered with my lawful right and obvious need to utilize the designated handicapped space. He vaguely hinted at the existence of ample indicia that professors had been allowed to usurp the space without benefit of either hang-tag or disability, which he mildly suggested tinged the incident of issuing me a ticket with a degree of irony that he presumed a jury would not find amusing. He ended his letter by stating that the campus construction worker who had reported me as "not looking disabled enough" to use the space, might consider whether he needed new glasses, or merely suffered from a lack of enlightenment about the law governing provision of accommodations to persons, such as myself, entitled to receive them.

I am not certain if Mr. Goodwin's letter turned the tide, or if the article on the front page of the University News did the trick, or both. One way or the other, the ticket found itself dismissed, and I resumed use of the space, in which I parked, daily, until I graduated in May of the following year.

Yesterday, as I entered the building where my office is located, a client of mine exited. *Hello Ms. Corley!* he sang, always a cheerful way to be greeted. I smiled and nodded my head towards a sleek black car parked in one of two designated curbside handicapped spaces without benefit of proper plates or placard.

*Not yours, I hope?* I asked him, and he shook his head.

*I'm worried about the driver,* I remarked. He raised his eyebrows. *Driving around blind, he must be,* I concluded, and my client laughed.

We talked about his case for a few minutes, and parted. I went into the building, and greeted our long-time receptionist, with my daily request that she reconsider going back to school and stay with us instead. She declined, as usual, and my day rolled into its beginning.

Now the morning surrounds me, with its buzzing lawnmowers, the slight drone of a small plane, and the flutter of our American flag in the gentle breeze. This is the last weekend of my son's summer occupancy of our home. I half-suspect that it is also his last summer in Kansas City, for I know he longs to find something exciting to do, in exotic ports, between junior and senior year. In a little while, I will take him to buy shoes, and try to impart a pearl or two of wisdom over a mocha latte. But for now, I will take my moderately to severely disabled body back inside, and make another pot of coffee.

Mugwumpishly tendered,


Corinne Corley

# Saturday Musings, 07 August 2010

Good morning,

With a stout cup of French Market on the tiled table beside me, near the newspaper, overshadowed by the gardenia that I have yet to kill, I am again enthroned on my beloved porch. The heat has abated, at least for this morning, and the breeze wafts the American flag, lifting it to unfurl and stretch, and wave with a heady reassurance that time has only served to perpetuate.

My stubborn allegiance to my particular vices can be forgiven, I hope, as I raise my cup to a passing neighbor. I do not drink alcohol to excess; I've never been one for drugs, except the prescription kind; and I don't beat my child except with hopelessly maudlin metaphors.

I started drinking coffee at 17, during weekend stints at St. Vincent Psychiatric Hospital in St. Louis County -- the old facility, with a sweeping, wide driveway, Gothic turrets and frightening back hallways. I served as unit secretary for 3South, the acute ward. On Saturdays and Sundays through my senior year of high school and first year of college, I transcribed doctor's orders and served the clerical needs of the patient care staff, watching the truly ill wander the hallways and sometimes, climb the walls.

I have only to catch sight of a slender woman lighting a cigarette -- of old, in a restaurant or an office; but these days,

more often on the patch of concrete in front of any building --
to remember my favorite patient, and wonder where life has
taken her, with her anguish, and her desperation.

Her parents gave her the name of Sydney, and they told
everyone whom they met, including a scrappy little ward
clerk with a tumble of hair, that they had wanted a boy. Sydney's frame mimicked the thin body of an adolescent; she
wore her hair short, with a pale blond lock across her forehead. She favored body-hugging ribbed turtle neck sweaters
and hiphugger blue jeans.

During the time that I knew her, Sydney was in her early
twenties, and spent several months each year getting stabi-
lized on 3South. Our ward consisted of ten patient rooms, a
nurses' station, a dining room, and the back hallway where
the EST treatments took place.

The dining room stood at one end; the nurses' station,
where I worked, at the other. Between them, the patient
rooms flanked the corridor, five on each side; and in the corridor itself, clutches of chairs stood at intervals in a clumsy
effort to make the place look homey. Sydney paced from one
end of this confine to the other for most of the hours between
meals every day.

The aides placed breakfast in the serving trays at 8; lunch
at noon; and dinner at 5. Sydney went through the line and
took minuscule helpings of each offering, huddled in a metal
chair at a Formica table by herself to nibble at the tasteless
food, and then, greedily lit a cigarette. She pulled huge gulps
of smoke into her lungs, closing her eyes, holding each draw
as long as she could, then releasing it slowly, purposefully,
taking several quick breathes between drags of cigarette.

Her smoking fascinated me; my parents both smoked at
the time, but I did not, never would, and I could not understand her obsession. One afternoon, halfway between lunch
and dinner, I chanced to be returning from my afternoon
break and saw Sydney in the dining room. I don't remember
what caught my eye -- the peculiar cant of her head, perhaps;

or a fleeting look of restrained panic. I paused, standing outside the door, watching. I glanced at the house phone on the wall, prepared to summon help by calling a code if I needed to do so, but waiting, in case I did not.

Sydney walked, hesitantly at first but with a quickening pace, to the long table on which clean, unfilled serving vessels stood. Her hand slowly rose, suspended above the empty space where aides would later stack dishes for the next meal. I swear that I could see her take a plastic plate from a ghostly stack; and lift a spoon to serve a scoop of invisible green beans, then mashed potatoes, then a piece of gray meat vaguely reminiscent of steak. I narrowed my eyes and blinked; but the serving trays remained empty, the spoon nonexistent, the plate imaginary.

But Sydney carried it gently, gingerly, to the table and set it in front of her. She took up an unseen fork, and speared a bite, sliding it between her lips, and chewing. I shook my head, turning my gaze to each end of the hallway, hoping a patient aide would chance upon this scene. When I looked back into the dining room, she still sat, eating food that I could not see, from a plate that did not exist, with a fork that I could swear she held but which still rested in the buffet behind the locked door of the downstairs kitchen.

She finished and rose to take her plate to the bus station. Reaching towards the bin in which the dirty dishes were to be stacked by the patients, she released her hand and I will swear, to this day, that I heard the clatter of the heavy plastic plate falling onto others already there. Sydney turned, then, and saw me; I drew back, but I need not have worried. Her dance had its own choreography.

She sat again at the table and took out her pack of cigarettes. She drew one out with a smooth and practiced motion. Placing it between her lips, she leaned forward, and I could see the form of a patient aide not yet on duty, leaning to light the cigarette for her; and I watched the rise of her chest as she drew a long, unbroken swell of unseen smoke. Then she closed her eyes, and euphoria settled on her features as I jumped back from the sight, stunned, saddened, and suddenly, ashamed.

Much of my day consisted of transferring medication orders from patient charts to requisition forms. Hospital care has greatly advanced in its record-keeping aspects with computerization; but forty years ago, the pen and the three-page carbon-paper form served as the vehicles for communicating with the various departments of the hospital. Ostensibly, I did not need to read the patients' history to perform my duties, but that afternoon, I read Sydney's chart, and learned that her father only allowed her to smoke after she had eaten. I mentioned what I had seen to the head nurse, who shrugged her shoulders dismissively. Nothing surprised her. She did not even make an entry in Sydney's daily log, though knowledge of this behavior might surely had aided in her treatment.

Later that summer, Sydney came again to 3South but on a stretcher, strapped and submissive, probably sedated. She lay in her bed for several weeks before whatever she had taken or been given worked through her system, and then resumed her pacing, up, down, nurses' station, dining room.

Between my desk and the rest of the floor stood a dutch door. We kept the top half open and the bottom half shut, supposedly locked. On a late August day that year, I was transcribing orders from a stack of charts at my desk, unaware that the last nurse to leave for lunch had failed to latch the door behind her. As I tried to decipher one doctor's particularly nasty scrawl, a large drop of red, viscous liquid fell upon the page.

I looked up. Sydney stood over me, her wrists held out in front of her, blood dripping from puncture wounds up and down her slender arms.

*Sydney*, I said, *you are bleeding on my charts.*

*What should I do,* she asked, in a barely audible whisper, her eyes wide, her face blanched.

*Bleed somewhere else,* I snapped.

She moved, then, to the end of my desk, holding her arms over my waste basket. With only a small glance back at my work, with only a brief hesitation, I lifted the phone, to call the code, and then stood back while all hell broke loose.

My last sight of Sydney was of her eyes: large, luminous, not even pleading, just watching me, from the cart on which the code team had placed her, as they pushed back through the hallway, and furiously raced towards the medical unit, where tired nurses would try to stench the flow from holes created with the narrow end of a rat's-tooth comb.

The coffee has grown cold, forgotten beside me. The black cat came home a few minutes ago, with a new, disturbing gash in his neck. My son still will not let me get this creature fixed, and so he fights with anything that challenges his territory, and I am waiting for the day when he is not brushing up against my legs when I come out onto the porch to get my newspaper. I understand why Patrick insists that we not curtail his cat's true nature. But freedom has its price, just as captivity does; and I am sometimes unable to decide which is worse.

Mugwumpishly tendered,


Corinne Corley

# Saturday Musings, 27 August 2011

Good morning,

Last evening, I stood in my driveway chatting with neighbors from across the way, the husband of the two being a man whose mother still occupies his boyhood home five doors north of me. They live in a house that once belonged to his uncle. We traded pleasantries, and discussed the departure to an assisted living facility of another long-time block resident, who had been born and raised here, and on this very block. Johanna never married, never had children, and never left. She grew to old age seeing the world through the eyes of her nieces and nephews, and the children and grandchildren of her friends. Her family possessions were auctioned off while I vacationed in Michigan this past week.

My vacation lulled me into a hazy sense of well-being. I undertook no task more vigorous than washing dishes. I read four books by European crime fiction writers and one by an American. I walked on trails, both high and low, on the eastern shore of Lake Michigan in the resort where my sister-in-law has a cottage that's been handed down through her family for several generations. My son launched his new college year from Michigan, in a Blazer less loaded than in the previous two years, his dwindling requirements matching the predictions of his college's president at the convocation for Patrick's freshman class. I stood in the roadway as he left, and barely shed a tear. Life continues.

With the warm Michigan sun casting delicate rays on my face, I drowsed on the bench that faces the Lake on the beach near the cottage. I drifted in time, in place, with thoughts of my childhood swimming to the near-conscious portions of my mind.

When I was four, my parents loaded us into whatever station wagon my father had at the time for a trip to my mother's parents' house. I can't name the make or model of the car. I remember its color, sort of a muddy grey-green, and the rope attached to the back of the front seat which we gripped when my father accelerated. He never went very fast. The inter-state highways had not yet been completed, and the state roadways that we took to Gillespie did not require much in the way of speed. With Mom holding the baby, my brother Frank, and the other six kids in the bench seats behind my parents, we made our way over the Chain of Rocks Bridge into Illinois and eventually, to Nana and Grandpa's home.

We arrived late in the evening. No one stirred in the house. Groggy, grumpy and grubby, we filed out of the car and up the wooden stairs of their front porch. The door was not locked -- in those days, the soft, casual days of the late 1950's, no one feared intruders; we did not even have a key to our house until well into the 1970's.

My mother scattered us with various tasks. The older siblings helped the little kids into pajamas, guided our hands on toothbrushes, and herded us down into the living room for night prayers. We knelt for the closing of the day in a darkened living room. At home, we would have faced the statue of the Blessed Virgin Mary in her alcove on the living room wall; at my grandparents' house, I think we faced a crucifix. We began the rosary. *Our Father, who art in heaven, hallowed be thy name, thy kingdom come, thy will be done, on earth as it is in heaven...* Suddenly, a tall figure loomed in the doorway, and I felt a surge of panic in my chest. My father rose and moved with a rapidity of which I had not known him capable. I heard the harsh growling of male humanity, braced for catastrophe -- and then the room flooded with light.

My mother stood at the light switch, facing the front doorway. My grandfather, tall, broad and clothed in a green serge suit, holding a leather satchel, towered in the space near her, my father's hands clenched on Grandpa's wrist. Beyond this tableau, my small, blond grandmother hovered, confused, uncertain.

Relief coursed through my body and must have done its work in everyone else, for my father stepped back and the set of my grandfather's shoulders eased. *We didn't expect you until tomorrow,* he said, with a mixture of reproach and relief. He shook my father's hand, and my mother stepped forward to embrace each of her parents in turn. We children rose from our knees and rushed forward, our nightly obligation abandoned. When each of us had received a kiss and a hair-tousle, and felt the warm caress of our Nana's hand on our newly-washed cheeks, we climbed the stairs to bed, while my mother settled onto the couch with my baby brother in her arms.

I don't remember if it was that trip or a later one in which my brother Mark and I got to stay longer than the rest of our family. We flanked our grandfather as the car pulled out of the driveway, early, on a Sunday morning, and then Grandpa handed a bucket to my brother and a basket of sandwiches to me. We followed his long, tireless stride down to the creek, and snuggled beside him as he fished, casting time and again over his head with a practiced ease more beautiful than a ballerina's twirl.

We ate the sandwiches that Nana had made as a late breakfast, under the shade of a tree, as the sun climbed towards the mid-day sky. We only caught one fish, with each of us wrapping our little mitts around the rod beside my grandfather's large, gentle brown hands so we could say we helped. Mark carried the bucket back to the house and hung it on the outside spigot, the fish swimming in creek water, my grandfather promising to clean it so we could cook it for dinner.

When we came outside later in the day, the fish was gone. The bucket swung a bit, as though it had just been moved. Must have wanted to go back to the river, my grandfather told us. He probably jumped out and wiggled his way down the yard, to the creek. Mighty strong fish you kids caught! We had chicken for dinner instead.

The dust gathers under the dining room table, drifting in a haze of pet hair that I must eradicate. I have a couple of weeks of laundry to do, and a whole slew of e-mail to read. Vacation is over. Fall approaches. The world keeps turning.

Mugwumpishly tendered,


Corinne Corley

# Midweek Musings:
## Mourning, Wednesday, August 24, 2011

Good afternoon,

I spent an hour and a half at the Zion Grove Missionary Baptist Church today, slipping away after the first choir number and before the eulogies. Although I only knew the deceased young man by sight, what I saw and experienced at his funeral moved me with such force, that I found myself unable to remain in the church.

A thousand or more, maybe two thousand, mourners filed into the church beginning shortly before the scheduled hour for the visitation. The young man whose life reached a tragic and heroic end had died as he had lived: protecting others. He had given shelter to children whose mother turned to Samir Clark for help, and as he sheltered them, their pursuer fired into the apartment where Samir had been visiting family, on whose door the children's mother had knocked. A bullet struck Samir, and he fell, dying within an hour or so thereafter.

Samir attended my son's high school. His brother Akeem was in Patrick's class, and Samir was in the class behind Patrick. Patrick and Samir had a close mutual friend, by virtue of whom they had contact. Patrick shared with me that Samir always showed the greatest of courtesy and respect for him; Samir treated him with kindness on occasions when others did not.

I learned, in the week since Samir's murder, that he attained Eagle Scout last year; that he participated in a mentoring program, that he helped out in the same food drives in which my son and I had been volunteers for Patrick's four years at University Academy of Learning Charter School, and also that he gave his time and energy to four separate churches as a volunteer, crossing into two different faiths to do community service. After a year of college in Iowa, he had been recruited by, and was transferring to, a university in Tennessee where he intended to continue his studies in biology and play football.

This life cut short so soon, had been a life well spent.

As I sat on the aisle of the church, watching his friends, teachers, Scout leaders and others collect, listening to the music, I tried to imagine how I would feel if Patrick had been killed in this manner -- or, indeed, in any manner. I cannot begin to reach those feelings, so deep would they run, so anguished would I be. I felt myself overcome with empathy for those who were closest to this boy, this young man. And as I sat, reflecting, I heard the soft voice of the pastor asking us to stand to receive the family.

I rose, with a thousand or more others.

Through the back door, near me, came a beautiful woman, held up on either side by young persons who looked so much like Samir that I knew they must be his siblings. The woman raised her eyes toward the front of the church, and stepped slowly. Her white suit, with its full-length skirt, fell in soft shimmers as she slowly traversed the aisle, and tears steadily streamed down her cheeks. Her boy, her beautiful boy, lay under a spray of blue and white flowers at the end of that long, terrible walk.

Violence cannot be justified. While this violence seems to have been personal -- directed at the woman who sought refuge in the apartment where Samir's killing took place -- nonetheless, violence rampages through our society. I am sickened by its brutal aftermath.

I could not stay for the entire ceremony, not because I had other commitments, but because I am weak: An abundance of sadness cripples me, and I retreat from it. Though I am reverent, and I do believe in the existence of a divine entity, nonetheless, I do not take the message of joy and salvation as one which affords us sufficient comfort to prevent our tears of sorrow at a life cut short too soon.

After I left the funeral, I chanced to exchange emails with a court clerk whom I know to be a woman of gentleness. I shared my experience with her in a brief summary of the events that I had witnessed, and she indicated that she had read about Samir's death. *It makes you re-think your job as a parent, to want to cherish your children more,* she wrote. And I agreed.

But it also makes me re-think my job as a love's after-math attorney. It reminds me of the difference between things of true importance, and things over which my clients should not bicker.

The lives we are privileged to bring into this world demand and deserve our strictest attention. I realize that we, as lawyers, are not responsible for our clients' decisions as to priorities during a custody fight. But we can draw a line, and we can ask our clients to consider if the points over which they instruct us to argue are really important, or if, instead, we could work with our opposing counsel and parties to structure a truly better future for our children.

Perhaps -- just perhaps -- we can whittle away at the malaise in society that spawns the fury which results in the loss of lives, such as that of Samir Clark. And until such time as the sickness of society abates, we should cherish the children of this world, and hold them close -- lest they be torn from us, as this precious child was torn from his mother's loving arms.

RIP Samir Ali Clark.

Mugwumpishly tendered,


Corinne Corley

# Saturday Musings, 25 August 2012

Good morning,

My droid tablet rests on a wicker footstool. The high note of a sea bird reaches my old ears, penetrating the slight fog of a short night and the ever-present drone of tinnitus. Walls clad in the timelessness of pine surround me. I have arrived at the destination which drove me to work ten-hour days these last few months: Maryland Cottage, Epworth Heights, Ludington, Michigan.

I chose to travel by train. I settled into the wide, comfortable front row on the Chicago-bound train out of St. Louis after spending the night at the home of my brother- and sister-in law, my host and hostess in this land of sand and towering trees. Whit drove me to the station and had a quiet word with the counter-agent to ensure my safe passage from the crowded terminal to my seat, a journey made in a narrow tram driven by a relentless woman whose gritted teeth warmed my heart. A sister leopard.

A compact woman dressed in stylish jeans with turned-back cuffs settled into the seat next to me, but after the first stop, she left to find a spot that didn't face the way we had come. She said it made her dizzy. I did not mind. The passing scenery looked the same whether I watched it arrive or watched it flit past. I settled back into the width of the two-passenger seat, alone, undisturbed, finding myself releasing each breath with increasing comfort.

North of St. Louis, industry gave way to small towns with dingy houses and dented cars. My book fell from my hand, landing on my small duffel, its pages briefly rippling before they softly closed. I leaned my head against the glass and watched Illinois slip south.

Towns gave way to farmland, field after field of burnt corn, between which lay long expanses of the green vegetation that could only be soy. The desolate fields of dead stalks brought home the brutal reality of the midwest summer. We stopped in a small station, maybe Granite City, maybe further away, and I raised my cell phone to take a shot of a railway yard filled with rusting cars labeled "Corn Products." They'd become a taggers' paradise, these useless vessels. On the flat surface of one labeled "Corn Starch only," an artist had carefully painted three-foot letters announcing JESUS SAVES.

The dry land gave way to untamed vegetation as we continued northward, flanking the tracks on either side. Through gaps in the woods, I saw neat backyards with above-ground pools, vibrant blue against the verdant green. Church spires rose above the rooftops. An occasional car waited at the crossings, the drivers evident only in the glint of sun on their glasses or an arm dangling from an open window. At one intersection, several people had turned off their engines, and stood between their vehicles, chatting. They watched my window as though waiting for me, and I could have sworn one of them nodded in my direction.

After Joliet, there could be no doubt that we neared Chicago. Trees yielded to the rangy clutches of weeds adorned with discarded rubbish. I saw a long trail of what I took for film stretched in the spindly branches of second-growth pin oak. A movie someone no longer wished to watch; a documentary that disappointed its director; porn filched from the seedy backroom of a video store, thrown over the side of the viaduct. Who could say?

We pulled into Chicago an hour late which I did not realize until I retrieved my suitcase from the rusty tram that toted the disabled from track to terminal. My connection to Michigan still had three hours til boarding, so I hauled my belongings through Union Station and found a sandwich shop in the Food Court. I blew several days' carb allotment on a chicken panini; I went hogwild and did not tell the smiling man behind the counter to hold the cheese. *I'm on vacation,* I reasoned; or perhaps that was rationalization. Either way, the melted Swiss warmed my stomach and brought a smile to my face. Small indulgences.

I sat beside a woman briefing a young man on the niceties of employment at the Corner Bakery. I could not ignore the kind cadence in her voice, or the nervousness in his. She assured him that the many rules which she outlined would soon become second-nature to him; she gave him a little quiz and prodded him along on a few of the thornier questions -- such as, When is it okay to give your friends a discount (never) and what do I do if I am going to be late to my shift (call). I leaned across the six inches between our table and told her that I had rarely heard someone speak with such gentleness. I gave her one of my law firm pens and told her to call me if she ever needed a friend in Kansas City.

I watched wild pandemonium for the four o'clock northboard train, and realized that I would be trampled if a similar crowd gathered for the 5:20. I timidly approached the gate agent and identified myself as one of the less robust, and voiced trepidation at the thought of mustering myself to answer the pre-boarding call with a hundred Michiganders chafing at the bit. She released the long expanse of canvas strapping that blocked entrance to the back waiting area, and helped me roll my suitcase through the opening. I sat where she told me to sit.

A lady resembling a gypsy staggered around the area. By shameless eavesdropping, I learned that she had been found wandering in the station. When approached, she tendered a legitimate ticket, for a 7:30 train. The TSA folks determined that she had some impairment -- possibly neurological, possibly alcohol-induced -- and fetched her along to the gate from which she would later, presumably, depart. As I had been, she had evidently been instructed where to sit, but periodically succumbed to panic and approached anyone who would talk to her, including me, for reassurance. They finally brought two female agents to sit with her. She huddled into her chair, with black hair falling over her lacy blouse, long skirt draping over her legs, a suitcase and a large pocketbook beside her on the floor. I averted my eyes. I have my own moments of folly; I recognized hers and spared her the stare of a condemning stranger.

As we left the Chicago station, I plugged my phone charger into the outlet next to my seat and activated my wireless hotspot. I logged into my email, and learned that a client's child had been caught in a hotline of her mother relative to one of her half-siblings. I had just gotten temporary principal residence for this client, after his daughter's mother had taken her to California without leave or notice. Now, the Children's Division investigator had cautioned him not to let the child have the visitation outlined in our temporary order until the allegations of abuse of her half-siblings could be resolved. His short email asked what he should do. I phoned him; and followed with a call to the investigator. Then, convinced that I could do nothing more until Monday, I settled back into my seat and opened the Maigret trio that I had brought to read on the train.

My eyes drifted back to the window before too long. Now the pin oaks rose taller, and the narrow strip of parkway between the tracks and the frontage road had been tamed by county mowers. The churches seemed more plentiful, as did the above-ground pools. The fields held richer bounty.

My sister-in-law texted, *Where are you?* and after learning of my approximate destination, told me to watch for the Lake near the town of St. Joseph. I got my cell phone ready, one eye out the window, one on the pages of the Simenon novel. Soon, I let the book alone again, and gazed upon the roadways of the towns through which we traveled. The sun started its drift towards the horizon, bold bright light raising the sky. I shot a few frames of its brilliance and posted them to Facebook.

The conductor heralded the approach of the St. Joseph station, and I got my camera ready. But still, I missed the best shot, mesmerized by the wide expanse of Lake Michigan and the unbridled kiss of the setting sun on its grey surface. We pulled to a smooth stop. In moments, we left the town of St. Joseph, headed north to Bangor.

A sturdy man in the seat behind me rose to flirt with the young girl across from me. The two decades between them meant nothing in the happy isolation of the train. His jokes did not threaten her; nor did his over-friendliness alarm. The confines of a train have given license to travelers since tracks first laid upon the earth, long before an even greater freedom with the invention of electronic mail. You can be who you like on a train, for hours at a time: shyness yields to daring, a chronic frown melts with the rays of the setting sun.

The man left the car in Bangor, waving, calling out that we ladies should have a wonderful weekend. And then another text, another query, and I said, *We are almost there, can you hear the whistle? Not yet, came the answer.* I leaned down to gather my belongings.

An attendant helped me down from the train and guided me to the sidewalk. She asked if I was being met in the tone that paralleled that used by the agents to the drunk gypsy. I forgave her; forgiveness comes easier in Michigan. I assured her that someone would come for me, and just then, I saw the broad sweep of Virginia's arm from the curb beyond the station fence.

And now, I am here. The Lake lies in all its splendid permanence a few hundred yards below the porch in which I sit and write. The sun unfolds its sweetness over Ludington. I wear the Vera Wang pajamas brought to ward off the chillness of northern August mornings. I am alone; Virginia stirs on the second floor but she and I are the only people here. For the next few days, I will be accountable to no one.

We will take long walks in this beautiful place, and drive to the charming towns. I will send as few emails about work as I can. I know that some work must be done remotely; I am a bit concerned that I did not get August billing out before I left. But this is Maryland Cottage, the unexpected bonus that I got when I remarried -- the chance to spend a week each year lounging in wicker furniture, sleeping past six, and listening to the sounds of the Lake, which even from this distance fill the air.

Mugwumpishly tendered,


Corinne Corley

# Saturday Musings, 08 September 2012

Good morning,

After a day and an evening of standing, more or less continuously, on arthritic feet in cheap shoes, my toes complained far into the hours when I should have been sleeping. Vanity lulled me into believing that I could tolerate these cute little wedge sandals. So I wore them to court, and to breakfast with a friend at the incomparable Ginger Sue's where the biscuits are divine, for a full day of lawyering, and to the liquor store. Then I stood in them and greeted the steady stream of visitors to the opening of the newest art showing in Suite 100. By ten o'clock, I sat on the side of my bed, rubbing reddened toes and massaging Burt's Bee Balm into the balls of my feet. Ridiculous.

And instantly, without warning, my mind flies back to the single time that I tottered on three-inch heels. Rochester, Minnesota. 1980. My brother Frank's wedding. I have a few photos, yellowed, curling, in an album in the one box that escaped a 1984 apartment flood and the rising waters in my current basement, the year that river rats overtook Kansas City, when rain fell in unrelenting sheets, forcing the Little Blue River over its banks and into the inadequate storm sewers.

I wore a black print dress to that wedding, and stood in tall, cheap, black patent shoes on the arm of the man who squired me that year. As thin as I am now, back then, I weighed 25 pounds less. The Corley clan formed a ring at the center of the reception in the bride's parents' backyard, adult siblings and our parents, maybe a brother-in-law and a small grandchild or two. I cast a backward glance outside our closed circle, at my brother's new in-laws and their friends. I did not speak of the divide, but felt its cold depths.

I realized my father had drifted away and into the house. Some instinct pulled me after him. I found him sitting on a sofa in the living room, holding a wine glass. I sat beside him, searching for the right words to softly mutter, worrying that he might be drunk, hoping that he was not.

*Did I ever teach you how to hold a wine glass,* he asked me, without warning. My gaze fell on the stem that I held. *No, Pops,* I acknowledged. *You never did.*

He raised his right hand, dark wine shimmering through the crystal. I transferred my glass to my left hand and mimicked him. We laughed at my efforts to crook my little finger as he instructed. He spoke my name, urged me to try again, and I did, my hand poised in the same way as his. We sat, on the sofa, at the Reeves home, in the quiet of the living room, an ounce or two of wine and a couple of decades between us.

Weeks later, an envelope arrived at my apartment in Kansas City. I slid a half-dozen photographs from between two rigid pieces of cardboard. I shuffled through images of me and the boyfriend with whom I had, by then, parted ways in a flood of tear-drenched betrayal. My unknowing mother did not mean to wound me by sending those along. I hurried past them.

The last picture had been taken just at the moment when I had finally gotten what my father had been trying to teach me. My hand rises in a perfect mirror of his. We gaze at one another, my chin a delicate version of his own, my button nose reflecting his Irish profile. My curls fall to my thin shoulders. He wears a navy blue suit and a dark tie, and I wear my black dress, legs crossed at the ankle, feet clad in those ridiculous shoes, frail arm contrasting with his more sturdy one.

I have no other pictures of me with my father.

In another photo album, I stand in the dress I wore at my first wedding, caught unawares, fury on my face. *That man is NOT walking me down the aisle!* I had told my sister, at precisely that moment. Her hand rests on my arm. *Calm down,* she whispered. *He'll hear you.* I told her that I did not care. My brother Stephen would take my arm, and guide me past the congregated friends. *Just tell him.*

On a shelf in my office, my parents turn to smile at a photographer as they dance at some other child's wedding. My father's face shines. My mother's smile is sweet. There are no children in the picture. When I sit at my desk, I can study them, and I often do. I don't know what answers I seek. I am not even sure what questions I am asking.

This morning, the throbbing in my feet has subsided. The blisters look more painful than they feel. The offending shoes, discarded, look innocent. But I know better. I won't be fooled again.

Mugwumpishly tendered,


Corinne Corley

# Saturday, 10 September 2016

Good morning,

From an AirBnB in San Rafael, I search for pictures of my Mother to share on this, the ninetieth anniversary of her birth. I have few. I've scanned some; taken snapshots of others; and snagged a few from my sister Adrienne's Facebook page. Someone might have more but all I have sits in space somewhere, grainy and awkward.

But she cannot fade from my memory. Recently one of my siblings reminded me that Mom had her flaws -- and she did; we all do. She allowed our father to commit atrocities on us which had no name then but today would be considered felonies. While I understand what happened to her, and why she felt powerless to fight him, still, there it is -- leaving us scarred, damaged, different, disillusioned. Some of us rose above what we felt and saw; some of us sank below the muck and mire. None of us emerged from our childhood without a profound burden, however easily or awkwardly each of us learned to carry it.

However, my mother had magnificent qualities. She gave me many of them. She steadfastly endured, and I have leaned on her example through my own travails. Mother could skip one moment and hold a troubled child the next. Possibly this mercurial quality would be seen today as manic-depression, but I just thought of it as adaptability. She had little tolerance for inanity, or cruelty, or illogic. She protected her babies with an unparalleled ferocity in most realms, though at home, only by standing in the way of many of my father's blows.

At least, I remember her this way. Others might have their own images, their own memories, their own opinions. But I persist in my assessment. Lucille Johanna Lyons Corley stands tall in my mind. Not perfect, certainly. Irreverent, often. Tired -- most assuredly. But present -- ever present, and unwavering.

It took me nearly 37 years to successfully bear a child. My mother died six years before my son's birth. I mourn the fact that he never got to meet her. They would have had fabulous talks, Patrick and Lucille. They have much in common, including an inner gentleness that happily came out in his genes though they skipped mine.

My first pregnancy ended in a bloody mess on the floor of my mother's bathroom in late winter, 1977. At twenty-one, aimless and undirected, I would have been a terrible parent. But I had known the child inside for a month or so, and desperately wanted the baby even if I had no earthly clue what to do with it. I stood helplessly clutching the sink, pressing a wash cloth to my mouth to stifle the sobs. My mother knocked on the door. Mary, let me in, she commanded. When she saw my face, she folded me in her arms. She did not require a confession. She led me from the room, stripped me, found a nightgown, and settled me in my old bedroom without making me answer for my actions. I fell asleep with a cup of half-drunk tea cooling on a tray beside me. Though I went back to my apartment the next day, my mother's love followed me. I slept for days under my great-grandmother's quilt which Mother sent with me that morning. It carried the heavy fragrance of home: Mother's perfume, over-cooked-coffee, and a curious blend of Pine-Sol and talcum powder.

In one of my many wooden boxes at home, I have my mother's defense medals, the bracelet she made from the baby beads of her first four children, and some pin that could be a Boy Scout den mother award. I have little else of hers. But every fiber of my being carries her stamp. I would not be sixty-one and still relentless if I were not my mother's daughter.

In a little while, I will go to see the garden of a gentleman whom I met on my travels. I will stand among the flowers in this temperate climate, remembering another garden, in Jennings, which bloomed beneath the tender care of a half-Austrian, half-Syrian, girl from Gillespie. I will think of how much my mother loved her flowers, and her vegetables, and her children. I will not cry. She would much prefer that her memory linger in my smile.

Mugwumpishly tendered,


Corinne Corley

# Saturday Musings, 26 September 2015

Good morning,

A warning twinge often courses through my legs just before they collapse, and that happened today at 7:25 a.m., right
after I put the crystal cup of yesterday's coffee in the microwave and en route to the front door to check for our boycat
on the porch. I hit the floor just west of the piano, flailing for
a hand-hold, scraping a chair across the hardwood as I tried
to grab its seat and missed.

I lay on the floor for several agonizing moments before I
realized that I had stopped breathing. My mouth gaped open
but nothing emerged: Not sound, not an exhaled stream
of carbon dioxide, nothing. I've broken a rib, it's going to
hurt like hell but *BREATHE DAMMIT BREATHE!* my brain
screamed but still my lungs did not heave. Panic immobi-
lized me. My face started to numb; a cloudy haze rose around
me and I thought, *Jesus Christ Corinne, You can't die because
you fell and broke a rib, breathe woman.* With a great internal lunge, I pushed my chest out and felt a cough rise, and
a moment later, I lay on my belly gagging. Shards of something that felt like glass rip through my chest, signaling that
indeed, I'd probably broken a rib but by God, I had made
myself breathe.

And suddenly I whipped back in time to 1982. On 09
February 1982, a crazy (self-described) Persian in a VW
knocked me into the air, sending me catapulting three stories

above the Tivoli. I slammed down on his hood and through his windshield. Seven weeks and a surgery later, my mother and a social worker flanked my casted body discussing whether I should be discharged to my fourth-floor apartment or a rehab unit.

Social worker: *What if there's a fire while she's still in this cast?, gesturing as though towards a piece of rotting meat. How will she get out? She won't be able to get down those four flights of stairs.*

The rotting meat's mother: *You don't know my daughter.*

It turns out that without a court order, a social worker could not actually prevent me from leaving the hospital when medically discharged to do so. Perhaps my youth prompted me to stubbornly insist; perhaps I'm just the kind of person that rises to a challenge; perhaps my insistence foretold a later brand by a frustrated spouse of doing whatever the hell I wanted. Regardless -- home to the fourth-floor flat went I, the rotting meat, with only a landline and an unlocked back door to provide help if I fell.

A few days into my recovery, I hit the floor just inside of the locked French doors to my balcony. As my crutches slammed and skidded out of reach, I found myself grateful that they hadn't shattered the glass panes. They came to rest about ten feet from my position. I lay panting, trying to calm myself, shifting the heavy weight of the toe-to-hip cast on my right leg and the ninety-pound body around it.

Silence gathered in the air and settled. Somewhere in the building, a phone rang for several long minutes. I thought about the telephone in the kitchen and the one beside my bed, twenty-five feet away -- it might as well have been on the moon. Chance might bring a friend sauntering up the back stairs; my next scheduled visitor would come at ten in the morning. I contemplated lying on the floor for seventeen hours and decided that I needed to figure out how to stand.

I surveyed the living room. I had a green fake-leather recliner, two parlor chairs (badly in need of re-upholstering, I noticed), and a heavy wood coffee table that looked almost sturdy enough to bear my weight. It would have to do. I began inching towards it, lamenting the dust on my robe, hearing my Con-law professor's query to my mother early in my hospital stay: *Was it her good leg or her bad leg?*

My mother's reply echoed in my brain as I slithered across my floor: *I didn't know she had a good leg.*

*She doesn't. Nor good arms, and her torso isn't much better. But she's stubborn and she's determined and she's going to get off this floor.* Ten minutes later by the leering clock on the end table, she's made it to the coffee table and grasped its edges. You'd think hauling ninety pounds and a full-length cast eighteen inches off the ground would not be difficult but it can be. With a neurological system that inhibits the smooth cooperation of your muscles and a weakened, post-surgical state, the process defies that simple easy tug to vertical stance. But in the end, the disposition of which a Jackson County Circuit Court judge would one day take judicial notice as being *relentless* prevailed, and I hauled myself to a sprawled position across the coffee table and lurched far enough forward to get momentum and throw myself backwards into the recliner.

I started laughing, then, but the laughter quickly morphed into long jagged sobs. A wave of raw emotion washed over me. My body quaked. But then the quake, as all quakes do, subsided and I lay, shuddering, trembling, panting, and eventually, still.

A half hour later, I heard a clumping on the back stairs and felt the floor quiver under a rush of motion. Steve Hanlen and a friend roller-skated through my apartment, one holding a six-pack of beer, one holding a bag of take-out. Round and round the living room they skated, calling my name, scolding me for not rising to meet them, settling in my spindly chairs with their wild grins flashing.

We ate; they drank beer. Steve got me a glass of water and after we'd eaten, lifted me from the chair and helped me into the restroom. He asked if someone would come to assist me that night. I shrugged off his question and put my arms around him. Thank you for this visit, Steve, I whispered. He returned my embrace and did not speak. Then, me settled back in my chair, rubbish for the back dumpster in hand, the two of them clambered back down the fire escape and skated away.

Thirty-three years nearly to the day: I lay on my living room floor in Brookside and tried to figure out how to get myself vertical. I could have called for Jessica; I could have slid twenty feet into the dining room to drag my cell phone from the table. I told myself that I would do one of those things if I could not get up in ten minutes. I had no way of knowing when my deadline came. But years of being in this predicament helped me figure out a way to get off the floor. I scooted over to the couch, pulled the throw pillows down to the floor, wiggled on top of one of them, and then flipped my 115 pounds over to steady my broken artificial knee on the pillow. Thus padded, I willed my torso, now screaming from the surely-broken rib, onto the couch, and leveraged the top of my body to its cushioned surface.

From there, sitting was a cinch. Standing, not so much, but I could smell the coffee and so, eventually, quivering, nearly crying, I got to my feet and made my way towards the nectar of gods in my purloined crystal cup in the microwave.

Out on the porch, I thought about that awful commercial -- *Help, I've Fallen And I Can't Get Up.* I reflected on five pounds that I still have to lose to get to my ideal 110, and how much harder everything has become since I started gaining weight again. I lamented the loss of my landline with its phone-in-every-room. I drank warmed-over coffee; read the news of Mr. Boehner's resignation and the Royals' abysmal loss; and breathed.

About halfway through the comics, I decided that my rib is not broken after all. And that I had another good story to tell. I thought about Steve, roller-skating through my apartment on 43rd Street. I remembered the last time we got together, just a few months ago, at the 75th Street Brewery on one of his visits north from Texas. I wondered if I had ever told him how close he and his friend came to finding me helpless on the floor. I whispered, outloud, there on the porch, *Thank God he came!* and went inside for another cup of yesterday's Joe.

Mugwumpishly tendered,


Corinne Corley


*2022 Postscript: Steve Hanlen passed away on 16 April 2020. RIP, Steverino. The world will never be the same without you.*

# Saturday Musings, 29 September 2012

Good morning,

I lumbered through a brutal week and skidded to a stop last evening, my brain numb, my legs beyond hope, my ego dizzy from satisfying moments alternating with dark seconds when I doubted the virtue of my very existence. I cannot even say that I suffered being dragged from a coma each morning, because worry tore me from fretful dreams hours before the moment when KCUR would have slammed into my subconscious. I would flip the switch to prevent its awakening my spouse, and stumble down the stairs, where even the old brown dog seemed confused by my early rising.

My most recent trial sputtered to a close an hour or two before the end of the three days allotted by the court. Highs and lows of the event include my losing my temper and accusing the opposing counsel of lying -- and learning, on the resultant recess, that she in fact had not, leading to my apologizing on the record with a pompous air tempered only by its sincerity. At other times, that ignoble occurrence paled next to a fifteen-minute dance with the judge, ending in his apology, the next day, for seeming to treat me more harshly than my opponent -- an apology somewhat dampened by his insistence on blaming my ineptitude at phrasing objections, a qualification that I neither disputed nor begrudged. He had, after all, also reversed himself on a ruling that resulted in the striking of a long series of questions designed to impeach my client, questions that I knew were improper. He hasn't given his judgment in the case yet, having taken it under advisement, but I am left with a sinking feeling that his reconsideration of that legal point signals his intention to rule against me. Cleaner record, less chance of reversal on appeal.

On each of the three days of trial, I took my mid-day meal at a nearby cafe, with pleasant, aromatic coffee and warm, good food. On the first day, I spent the noon hour preparing my client for cross-examination for the third or fourth time, fearing that his self-righteous indignation would play as guilt. On the second day, I traded pleasantries with a witness whom my client had identified in the days before trial as knowing both himself and the opposing party, with whom I had traded voice mails. The forty-five minutes during the noon hour allowed only a brief assessment of any contribution that he could make to my client's tale, but I took a chance and used his testimony. Only time will tell if he played well, but he certainly broke the tension, sandwiched between a vicious cross-examination of my client and the sad, unimpeachable, quiet utterances of my client's father. At noon on the last day of trial, I talked at length with my client and his wife about a pending motion to interview the children, filed a couple of years ago by my predecessor, which I knew the judge wanted us to withdraw. I ate half a brownie, drank three strong cups of coffee, and convinced my client that his daughter had been through enough.

Early each morning, and at the end of each day, I made the hour journey from my home to the small town where the trial took place. I tried each of the available routes, finding varying degrees of traffic and construction. Regardless of how I traveled, the trip took the same amount of time, and afforded me the same views of long, sweeping fields, small clutches of farm buildings, the occasional Quik Trip and the battered vehicles of fellow commuters. I sipped coffee in the car, once from home, twice from QT, and ate breakfasts of protein bars and grapes while I traveled. My six decades sat heavily, awkwardly, like the lead shields draped against me in my child-bearing years when I had to have X-rays. Adjusting the car seat had no impact on my comfort. I'm too old for this, I told myself, as the miles fell behind me. Too old to rise before five o'clock for anything but bird-watching; past my prime; on the downhill slope.

On the second day of trial, on a stretch of state highway resembling so many others, I experienced the peculiar sensation of confusion, a momentary lapse of coherence, when I could not have said whether I was, in fact, coming or going. I continued forward only because I knew that I had journeyed without stopping and so must be on the correct route. A mist hung over the fields on either side of me. I could have been anywhere, at any time: Newton County, Arkansas, on my way to Fayetteville; south of Kansas City, traveling to Memphis; or passing the long stretch of green before the "Watch For Fog" bridge, in mid-Missouri, on my way to St. Louis.

A trial is often the anti-climax for the lawyers conducting it. The hours, and days, and weeks before the judge raises the curtain by uttering the first words of the record consume the advocates who stage the play. By the time I unpack my trial bag, unloading files and tablets onto the counsel table, I have already played each scene a thousand different ways. I have already analyzed my performance, and relentlessly critiqued the evidence on both sides, as well as every decision that I have made since my client signed our contract. In half of the scenarios, the judge rules in my client's favor; in half, against us.

The truth, as the whole world knows, lies between what one side wants and what the other fights to claim. Family law cases have no clean resolution. No jury eyes the witnesses and says, "Find for the plaintiff, award fifty thousand dollars", and no judge's gavel ends the dispute. No check can be written to satisfy anyone but the lawyers who shuffle papers. There are no winners; and there are too many losers.

I used the extra hours on Thursday to settle back into my office routine. I drove the hour into town and parked in the space behind my customary place, behind a car with no handicapped license or placard, the driver of which obviously has no regard for the rights of disabled people or the sanctity of the law. I photographed his license plate with my too-Smart phone, uploaded it to Facebook with a caustic comment, and dragged my crippled legs from the cramped confines of my little Vue. Thirty minutes later, nursing a cooling cup of coffee, I answered my assistant's request that I talk to a couple of clients in the conference room with a long, heart-felt groan. But I went, and forty-five minutes later, as I shook the hand of a young father and Air Force corpsman who only wanted my assurance that I would fight for his right to see his son even when he went on active duty, I felt no remorse.

Now the weekend has already given me a pleasant dinner, a trip to the book store, and nine hours of much-needed sleep, albeit with an extra hit of pain medication to quell my protesting, lily-white spastic legs.. By and by, I will, with some reluctance, start the weekly house-keeping, but for the moment, I am content to pretend to read the headlines of the morning newspaper and pour myself another cup of Joe.

Mugwumpishly tendered,


Corinne Corley

# Saturday Musings, 06 October 2012

Good morning,

The paper lies idle beside me, no headline worth the effort to turn its pages. A text back and forth from my neighbor shows that I am not the only one awake and deploying electronics this morning. I await a reply from my son as to whether we can discard the old electric street light that he scavenged years ago and which now resides on an otherwise useful shelf in the basement. It's Dumpster Day in the neighborhood.

Halloween draws near. A cluster of costumed boys in varying sizes fills an entire wing of my mind. Batman, Ninja Turtles, faceless zombies and vampires mingle, all incarnations of my son and the two or three boys from whom he was inseparable in the trick-or-treating years. No princesses for this boy-mom, as I came to be known. Eyeliner streaked on a small cheek mimics dirt and unshaven jowls. They gathered candy in pillow cases and pennies for UNICEF in a colorful canister. We decorated the front porch with cobwebs and candlesticks, pumpkins and witches. We put a significant dent in the goody bowls in three separate neighborhoods, starting and ending at my home. The tired, satisfied heads of my son and his friends nodded over the collection of treats until they fell asleep and I could turn out the lights, set the alarm, and collapse. Where they walked, I trudged behind them, with the flashlight, my car keys, and an extra paper bag, just in case someone needed an emergency candy receptacle.

We don't even give out candy any more at my house. A few years ago, I began to notice that the trick-or-treaters after seven o'clock did not even bother with costumes and stood inches above my height. I started extinguishing the porch light earlier and earlier, to fend off kids who had no connection with my neighborhood, whose parents drove them farther and farther afield, hoping for a bigger and better haul. Now I only buy Halloween candy for the dishes in our office, and if I go out on Halloween, I don't leave the porch light burning, preferring to stumble up the stairs rather than face the destruction that my unanswered door might invite.

Before my cynicism drove me to abandon the dispensing of treats, a particularly small ballerina knocked on my door, holding a plastic pumpkin, gazing the three feet up to my face with unbridled awe. Her father stood behind her, down on the steps, letting her venture to the door by herself but hovering close enough to protect. He looked familiar, like someone I had seen in a different guise, not that of proud papa. As I let his little pink-clad daughter rummage through the bowl of candy, I mentioned my impression. A grin dawned. *Oh, yes ma'am,* he assured me. *I came to your house on Halloween myself for years. You always had the best candy. My parents lived over on Charlotte, and I remember you so well! I just had to bring my baby here!* Charlotte is the street behind my house. A neighborhood kid then, grown, raising the next generation.

I gave him and his daughter a smile of my own, one that I had been saving for a special occasion. As he hoisted the little girl on his shoulder and turned to descend to my sidewalk and out to his car, the little girl raised her hand, spreading her five delicate fingers in a definite wave. Then she rested her head on her papa's shoulder and closed her eyes.

Autumn reclaims my neighborhood. The heat-stressed hollies in my front yard are brown and straggly, and the maple leaves began to turn too soon. But the earth has raised itself from the slump of summer and shimmied its shoulders. Cool air soothes the bedraggled gardens. On the surrounding porches, new pots of spider mums replace the drabness of dead annuals in their dusty containers. October has come, and will soon reach its end, the brief fall giving way to winter all too soon. I have already started running the heat, and unpacked my winter garments, for the nineteenth time since I bought this house. And, though I won't light the porch for Halloween, it will be crowded with ghosts nonetheless, and the echoes of tricksters clamoring for candy from the best house on the block.

Mugwumpishly tendered,


Corinne Corley

# Saturday Musings, 12 October 2013

Good morning,

The begonias on my porch have burst forth in bloom again. Each spring, I trot off to Soil Service and return with a flat of the carefree plants. I dig my hands in my huge bag of soil and gently set each small begonia in a new bed of dirt, in a clean pot. I fill my old plastic watering can and soak their roots. They boldly raise their leaves towards the sun, unfurling their colorful adornment, until late July, when the Missouri heat scalds their greenery and shrivels the delicate petals. But this year, only my shy little gardenia bush withered; the potted plants grew tall, and full, and sent out blossom after blossom. I sit looking at them, and thinking of the most recent gardener in my life, my mother-in-law, Joanna Mitchell MacLaughlin, who slipped away from us this week.

She spent the last six months of her life in comfort at a facility aptly called The Sweet Life. Though at first, she wanted only to go home, nonetheless she felt the room to be comfortable and pretty. She would pat the table which stood under the window, and gesture to the matching chairs and the wide dresser. Jay bought these things for me, she told me, time and again, as though perhaps I might have forgotten. And he bought that lamp, too, she would add, and smile at me. The smile told me, I am loved, you know; Jabez MacLaughlin loves me. She didn't need to say the words. The sweep of her hand, encompassing the tangible  proof of his adoration, said them for her.

I tried to visit her as often as I could. The "speech therapist" -- a Sweet Life code word for the folks who prompted her to strain her failing memory -- urged us to keep her mind stimulated. I tried bringing her books in the genre we both enjoyed, but she could not focus. Then, one clear blue Saturday, I went to Suburban Lawn and Garden, and found a willing clerk. I want to put together a portable gardening kit, I told him. I want to garden with my mother-in-law, but we only have a four-foot table on which to work, and one window sill's worth of space. The man smiled, and pulled a cart over. He told me to push, and walk with him. He found a window box, some sturdy hand tools, a good-sized bag of soil, and a flat of begonias. I added gloves, and a small, long-spouted watering can, and away I went.

I loaded it all on the same dolly that I use to take my trial bag into the courthouse, a small silver carrier which unfolds to the perfect size for one banker's box. I wheeled it into the Sweet Life and past the wide-eyed, covetous glances of the other residents. I made my way to Joanna's room, where she sat in a chair, gazing out her window.

She turned her eyes towards me and the corners  of her mouth curled upward. But the light in her eyes turned radiant when her glance fell on my burden. You've got begonias, she exclaimed, and extended her hand towards my little four-wheeler. I hauled the plants, and the window box, and soil, and the shiny new tools, to the dining room table that Jabez MacLaughlin had bought for his beautiful bride. I spread some newspaper down to protect the table's surface, remarking that the paper probably wasn't good for much else, so bad had its writing gotten. Joanna laughed, a small, gentle sound; but she did not join me in criticizing anything, even the local rag.

I situated the supplies within Joanna's reach. She looked over the pile without speaking, as though assessing and planning. Then she picked up the canvas gloves and pulled them over her slender fingers. She turned her eyes towards me and gestured for me to put some rocks into the bottom of the container. I held open the bag of soil and she took a handful of good rich dirt, and covered the stones. She eased the plants from their plastic cups, aligning them in a row within the long rectangle, on top of the first layer of soil. To that point, she had been sitting; but she seemed impatient with my manner of doling out the dirt. She raised herself from the chair, and dug both of her hands deep into the bag, then changed her mind. She lifted the bag and dumped a generous mound of dirt, enough to surround the flowers. She patted the mound level, added more, then looked up at me. And at that precise moment, I took her picture: Joanna -- making a tiny but lovely garden, on the table that Jabez MacLaughlin got for her.

A few minutes later, her fatigue overcame her and she lowered herself into the chair. She let me fill the watering can and bring it to her. It took both of her arms to lift it, but she soaked the soil, then pressed it firmly down around the slender stalks. I hoisted the finished box to the window sill, situating it under the stained glass piece that Joanna's sister Patt gave her, which dangled from the window lock. I cleared away the debris, and repacked the gardening tools. She sat by the table, with a sweet, contented expression molding her delicate features. I like to garden, she remarked, her face glowing. We sat in silence for a while, surrounded by the flowers and, restored to their places on her table, the photographs of her daughter Virginia, her son Jim, her grandchildren, and her beloved Jabez. At that moment, we had no need for words.

I only knew Joanna for a little more than four years. Like all great ladies, though, she taught me much. She smiled whenever anyone came into the room. When she first saw you, she would invariably mention something pleasant -- some little thing about you that she remembered: a class you were taking, a new job you had, or something she remembered doing with you. She offered you something refreshing, to eat, or drink; and listened to your stories with an air of interest. She'd tuck those stories away, and trot them out the next time she saw you, to ask you how things were, and whether you had managed to succeed at something you mentioned intending to try. And you would go away thinking, what a nice lady, and for the rest of the day, you would wear the smile that she had given you. And that, I would say, is the mark of a wonderful person.

Mugwumpishly tendered,


Corinne Corley

*In Memory: Joanna Mitchell MacLaughlin,*
*08/17/30 - 10/08/13. Rest easy.*

# Saturday Musings, 20 October 2012

Good morning,

It's dark, darker than a Saturday should be, the kind of creeping darkness that holds the threat of chill, and dampness. I have awakened early because I have a journey planned, and a few last minute chores await.

Nothing much happened on Friday. I got little done at the office, enjoyed lunch with my father-in-law, and sent out October billing a week or two early; in some cases, September billing, a week or two late. Around 4:30, having had enough of being responsible for the lives of people with whom I have only a contractual connection, I abdicated. Throwing my bag on the back seat to join the clutter of two weeks' worth of court jackets dangling from hangers, I started south, to Brookside.

A text message from my son distracted me. It said something about money, one of the few subjects that can startle me into instant action. I clicked the button that rings his cell phone, which no doubt rested in the change well of his Blazer as he traveled from St. Paul to Greencastle by way of a toll road. I drew from his reluctant voice, the fact that nowhere between Indiana and Minnesota, had he found a Bank of America, so his paychecks still had not been deposited. I levied a few salty measures of motherly castigation on his head, before agreeing to transfer some funds from my account to his. He endured my admonishments for longer than I expected, then suddenly, tellingly, with artificial urgency, spoke a familiar phrase: *I'm going through a tunnel, Mom; I'll have to call you back.*

My car continued its descent to the Plaza, towards Brush Creek, our local storm sewer with its odd concrete walkways. But my mind drifted back to another phone call, in 1977, when a younger version of Patrick's mother stood in the kitchen, talking to her own parental unit.

I had paced back and forth in the galley kitchen of my shotgun apartment, holding the receiver with its long spiral cord, wedged between my shoulder and my ear. *Uh huh,* I muttered, time and again. *Yeah, yeah Mom, I will. Yeah, Mom, I know.*

Suddenly, I looked down at the floor. *Oh, Mom, I gotta go; the cat's on the telephone wire.* I hung up the phone, scooped my little kitten into the crooked of my arm, and went out onto the porch. A few minutes later, the phone rang. *What was that supposed to mean,* my mother snapped. *Really, Mary?* "The cat's on the wire?" I laughed nervously, but the silence at the other end of the phone signaled that apology, not laughter, should be forthcoming. *I'm sorry. . .really. . .I'm sorry.*

She forgave me, of course; and for the next eight years, until her death, when either of us had grown tired of a conversation, we would trill: *Oh, sorry! Gotta go! The cat's on the wire!* She would chuckle, deep, resonate, and I would answer with my higher voice, more of a giggle. We would say our goodbyes until the next time. *Oh, sorry! Cat's on the wire!* and neither of us harbored any resentment.

I vividly recall my mother's telephone voice. I could lift a receiver right now, dial her number, and expect to hear the same cadence. And I have replayed, over, and over, and over, the last telephone call I had with her: *Oh, Mary, the X-Ray technician broke my arm. Can you please come home?* And I did. I couldn't do much for her; drive to St. Louis every weekend to spell my sister and my brothers; sit by her side, endlessly playing Willie Nelson albums and the New World Symphony, while I read from her favorite novels or the Book of Ruth.

One afternoon, she turned her head towards me, and focused her liquid brown eyes on my face. She might have been searching for something; she might have been wondering where she could find herself in my pale Irish skin and my own blue-grey eyes. But maybe not: for she whispered, with a ghost of a smile, *The cat's on the wire,* just before she fell into a sweet, simple sleep.

I watched her for a while, the rise and fall of her thin chest. Then I pulled her bed jacket closer around her shoulders, and just sat, whatever book I had been reading falling idle to the side of the bed. And the room quieted down around us, around my mother and me. I don't remember when Patrick started using the oncoming tunnel dodge to terminate a call of which he has grown weary. But this time, this Friday, at the end of a strange week filled with missed cues, anxious clients, and impatient judges, I felt the warmth of a mother's peace settle on my face as I laughed, telling him to drive carefully through that tunnel, and to call me when he reaches the other side.

I'm going to Arkansas. Some friends from my Fayetteville days have invited me down. Last night, I finished washing the towels and bought a new coat. There's nothing to keep me from this journey. I'm going alone, down 71, to the place where my child was born. I haven't been there in fifteen years. As I glide into town, with the gentle slope of the Ozarks on my left, I am sure that the changes will astound me. I don't think there are any tunnels, though you never know. I am keeping the phone fully charged, just in case.

Mugwumpishly tendered,


Corinne Corley

# Saturday Musings, 23 October 2010

Good morning,

I stand on the porch this morning, plastic-clad paper at my feet, white cat on the far end of the wheelchair ramp railing, and gaze above my head into the pitched roof of my porch. I draw in a long, cleansing breath of rain-washed air and listen to the faint stirring of someone's wind-chime, high and gentle.

Hearing confounds me. The gentlest note in an elevated range might reach me, but a murmured endearment at a low register will not. At times when ambient noise scrambles to claim my focus, I hear nothing and everything. A voice can carry down a corridor with crystal clarity; and a whisper beside my ear can be incomprehensible.

The man who built the porch on which I stand has a commanding voice, once familiar to local theatre audiences and radio listeners, resonant and sure. Remembering its timbre, I draw another gasp of air and find myself standing not on my familiar porch but in the large kitchen of our home in Jasper, Arkansas.

The Buffalo River ran behind that house, at the bottom of a sharp drop at the back edge of our property. We rented the place. It stood on the northwest side of the town square, next to City Hall. We selected it because of its large underground garage, where saws, lumber, and the tools of a carpenter's trade could be stowed and used.

He and I had been married for six months when we came to live in that small town. We shared its few scraggly streets with five hundred sixty-four people by the most recent census count, though six-hundred eight tapped into the water line. Our house stood one spot beyond the city treatment plant, and on water purification days, the chlorine smell made me gag and I could not shower.

By the summer of 1988, I knew that country life held no charm for me. I struggled with the vagaries of small town practice. Though our house sported a separate entrance to the room which I used for an office, everybody came to the front door and sat in our living room to share their stories. I wrote their wills; and cobbled together the shambles of their finances after divorce, and when I could not stand the mundane though poignant demands on my talent, I volunteered to represent people in chancery court whose lives had come undone.

Chester, my then-husband, did freelance set design that year. It had not gone well. We left Little Rock when a change in administration at the theatre company which had lured him south resulted in the wholesale replacement of the entire staff, including their most recent hire, my husband. So to Jasper we came, where he owned mountain property and had always wanted to relocate, and we staunchly tried to settle into life so different from any we had known that our folly must have been apparent to everyone but us.

And so we made our way to that summer, when we could sleep with doors and windows wide, catching the wind that lifted the day's stale air and sent it on its way. The neighbor's rooster awakened us before we might otherwise have wanted to face the daylight, and we pulled ourselves through the silence of spoiling marital discord surrounded by the bold beauty of the Arkansas Ozarks.

I frequented the library in the basement of City Hall. Though I had read most of the novels on its shelves, I found a few that bore re-reading. I grew to know the mayor, a woman whose face I can still picture but whose name I cannot recall. She ran the city of Jasper with thoughtful delicacy, and that summer, her four-year-old granddaughter visited her at City Hall most afternoons, playing on the tile of the reception room, searching for pretty rocks on the edges of the small ravine, thoughtless and simple in the ways of the very young.

On one such day, I hovered in the kitchen, disturbed by silence, wishing I had friends to visit or pubs to frequent, music to hear, smoky air to inhale. As I shifted the pans around, waiting for inspiration regarding our dinner, I heard my husband's voice, calm, but urgent, with the pitched resonance of controlled projection: One word, *Corinne*.

I tilted my head, listening to the ever-present tinnitus in my bad ear, straining, wondering if my lonely imagination had created the call. Then his voice came to me again: *Corinne, come now. Corinne. Corinne.*

I started towards the door when he spoke a third time, from within a hollow block of stagnant summer air: *Come slowly. Bring the .22.*

One learns, in the country, in the mountains, to keep the weapons loaded. The children are taught to clean, load, and carry a rifle, and to respect both the power and danger of guns. Though I had been raised in St. Louis, I had lived in Arkansas long enough to understand the foreboding portent of Chester's directive, and I got the Winchester and exited the house, catching the screen door behind me so that its closing made no sound.

He stood outside the perimeter of our yard, in the driveway of City Hall, his back to me. In front of him, four or five feet away, crouched the mayor's small, delicate granddaughter. I moved, with unaccustomed stealth, barely stirring the dry grass beneath my feet.

As I drew close to him, I saw the creature that hovered between my husband and the little girl: A snake, born of the ancient lands around us, foreign to the cracked concrete, as lost and as frightened as the child whom it faced. Poised, considering, frozen in the silent moment that it had taken me to respond to my husband's urgent summons.

Chester raised his arm and reached behind his body at the same instant that I lifted the rifle and placed it into his hand. With swift, noiseless motion, he brought the rifle to his shoulder, squinted, took aim. In that last, long second, with the girl's pale blondness rigid in the summer air and me stock-still behind my husband, the snake swiftly shook its rattle and raised its head, whether to strike or make a better target, I cannot say, for just then, my husband squeezed the trigger, and the snake fell dead.

Chester dropped the rifle and stepped across the endless span of time and space to the child, bringing her body into the span of his arms, over the fallen foe, whose only real crime had been to venture into a world in which it had no genuine chance of survival. I released the breath that I did not know I had been holding, and dropped my shoulders. Bending, I retrieved the gun, and went back into the house, leaving Chester to tell our mayor how close she had come to one of the most brutal lessons of country life.

Twenty-two years later, I stand on the porch that Chester built, whose design had been conceived and nurtured by my second husband, and approved by an architect friend. I glance down at the concrete surface of the floor beneath my bare feet, but nothing lies in front of me other than a trampled cricket. A passing car honks, and I hear the skitter of the small animal frightened into motion by the sudden sound. My reverie broken, I turn, and go into the house, where the coffee has finished brewing, and the computer awaits me.

Mugwumpishly tendered,


Corinne Corley


188

# Saturday Musings, 27 October 2012

Good morning,

A small victory: I slept all night without waking. Feeling refreshed is too much for which to hope, but staying asleep for eight hours signals that at least, my conscience rests.

Grey crowds my face, beaten back only by the skillful hand of a kind stylist. I wrench my elbow, and groan for hours, days, weeks, no longer cheerfully rebounding from every spill. I manipulate my neck and feel a crunching that causes me to wince. Middle age claims me; I stand on the brink of the downhill stretch.

Into this state seeps a trigger for memory. My son's friend Alex Thompson, who has written a screenplay about his Greek grandmother in which Olympia Dukakis has agreed to star, sends a tweet into the happy abyss of the internet: *I've written about my yiayia -- send me stories about YOUR yiayias.* Oh, memory: you rise to haunt me.

I'm back in a ranch house, the first built in the subdivision called Lake Knolls, sitting on the bend of a highway halfway between Chatham and Springfield, Illinois. My nana, the strongest, surest, finest woman that I have ever known, then or since, has been felled, slowed, bested, by a series of gruesome strokes. She stands in the living room, flanked by a worn recliner, a pale-colored sofa, and a console television, in this summer of my thirteenth year, one leg in a brace, her arm lifeless and withered by her side, and tries to tell me something.

*Ddddd-er, ddd-eer,* she stammers, my Nana, the woman who taught me to always put my best foot forward, who bought me shoes that I could be proud to wear, who read to me summer, after summer, after scary summer, when my brother and I had been sent to the safe harbor of her Gillespie home. *Dddeerrrrrr -- ddddeeerrrrr!!!,* her urgent demand.

It wasn't fair that I should be tasked with trying to determine what Nana wanted that day. My grandfather had gone to work; I don't know where my brother had gone, possibly for a walk, down to the scraggly banks of the nearby creek, at the end of a dirt road beyond the cornfield next to our grandparents' home. I glanced around, desperate, worried, fearful. What does she want, I asked myself, a cold knot forming in my stomach. Still she stammered, stuttered, a frenzied look in her eyes, pleading with me to figure out the word that escaped her.

I couldn't. I turned, pretending that I didn't know, didn't understand, that Nana needed something. I'm going to my room, I told her, with a false, cold cheeriness. I went into the den in which I had been sleeping, where the fold-out couch had been restored to the guise of seating and my small suitcase held a handful of books brought from the public library at home. I grabbed one of them and curled into the farthest corner of the sofa, scrunched against the arm, under the window. I opened the book to a random page and held it resolutely against my bent knees, unable to read for the tears forming in my eyes.

I heard the painful steps of my grandmother pulling her ravaged body through the hallway to the bathroom. What followed could only be the sound of a person with just one functioning arm rummaging through a medicine cabinet. Grief stamped my face, dampened my cheeks, spilled to the surface of the book. I threw it across the room, my chest heaving with a terrible mix of self-righteousness and self-loathing.

When I went back out into the living room, Nana stood in the place where I had left her, holding a bottle from which she drank without benefit of spoon or dispenser. Her three-pronged cane discarded against the chair, she teetered, unstable, her internal resolve the only thing keeping her upright. I crossed to stand beside her, and put my own thin arms around her, lowering her heavy frame into a chair, easing the bottle from which she had drunk from the tight, frantic clutch of her one good hand. A brief glance at the bottle: castor oil. My disgust with my own obstinate unwillingness to help the woman who had given me so much rose in sickening waves. I sat on the arm of the chair, one arm across her shoulders. Neither of us spoke.

Late that night, with the cool summer air surrounding us on the patio, my grandfather calmed me with his deep, low, soothing voice. *It's okay, little one, don't worry,* he told me, holding me, petting my arm, singing the songs with which he had lulled me to sleep in the long-ago days of my babyhood. My Nana had gone to bed, her body ravaged and her bones weary, and my brother sat with us in the dark, having no words to help me forgive myself for failing our grandmother.

I remember the last time I saw Nana. My mother had come to retrieve me after my annual summer visit. I would have said it was 1973, though a quick search of the Social Security death records tells me otherwise. In any event, we left Nana and Grandpa's home while my grandfather was not there; I'm sure he was at work. Nana had cajoled my mother into cleaning her house, sweeping the patio, and taking some leftovers to eat in the car. She stood at the door, waving her one good arm, and my mother let the engine idle. *Do you think she knows we are leaving?* I asked.

My mother shook her head. We waited, and Nana smiled, the sweet smile that I had always seen on her face, for all of my life. *She knows something,* my mother finally remarked, and we backed out of the driveway.

A short while after my grandmother died, my grandfather bought a new car. I had gone to stay in the dorm room to which I was assigned for that fall semester. We planned a family Sunday dinner for the next day, and my grandfather was to come down to St. Louis. I felt uneasy, unsettled, and I dreamed of my Nana. I saw her, sitting in the back of Grandpa's new vehicle, her face smooth, her arms strong, her eyes clear. *Tell Lucy not to cry,* she said. *Tell her I'm just fine now.* Lucy -- my mother. The next day, I did as I had been told. My mother nodded once and did not cry.

Mugwumpishly tendered,


Corinne Corley

# Saturday Musings, 05 November 2011

Good morning,

From an old rocker in my living room, as Friday drew to a close, I watched a neighbor and her husband walk by. Their stride has slowed in the last few years, and they took several minutes to pass my window. I stood and crossed the room to stand at the window for a better view. I noticed the wife's hair has grown to a lovely shade of silver, and the husband wears a cap similar to one my grandfather might have worn, decades ago. In years past, this couple zinged past my window on their bicycles, she ahead, he behind, and groceries bobbing in a basket perched in front -- sometimes on his bike, other times on hers.

Even more than the thickening of grey in my own hair, and the tightening of my own joints and muscles, the changes to this pair of devoted lovebirds mark the passage of time. For a few months, in 2008 or 9, the husband took his evening bike ride alone. I learned through the neighborhood grapevine that the wife suffered some undisclosed ailment. Since then, I have not seen them on bikes but they still take their evening constitutional, on foot now, faithfully.

I expect to see one of them alone some day, and I will know that their lives have come full circle.

The particular oddness of my watching these neighbors lies not in my voyeuristic monitoring of their lives' devolu-

193

tion, but in the fact that the woman of this couple went to my law school, graduating in the class behind mine. Yet I have never spoken to her in all the years that we have lived within blocks of one another. I know her name, and yet I do not call it. I made an effort to do so, once, about fifteen years ago. I greeted her as my son and I walked in front of her house with our Beagle in tow. Her eyes evaded mine. I do not know if she failed to recognize me, or knew me but did not wish to engage. I tell myself that I am respecting her preference for solitude.

Two blocks north of me, a house stands empty. Its occupant, a woman named Johanna, has moved to a retirement facility. The one-story bungalow had been her childhood home. She never married, never had children, never took a room mate or a boarder. She, too, walked every day, greeting my son and me, hailing the other walkers and the men who mowed their lawns. I often wondered what she thought of the changing block. I spoke to her only in superficial tones, about the weather, my son's growth, the relative state of her infirmity and mine. She walked on her own for years, and then with a wheeled walker and finally, with a minder. One day she did not appear; a few weeks later, I saw an ambulance at her house. Now the "For Sale" sign signals her first and last departure from the home she occupied for eight decades.

In Jasper, Arkansas, town of 562 (603 on the water line), I represented a friend's grandmother when she sold her house and moved into a nursing home one county north. Everyone on the block helped me pack her belongings. With my client ensconced in a wide rocker made by her deceased husband, the wives came one after another, with gift-wrapped trinkets which might never get used -- hand-embroidered handker-chiefs, small jars of home-made preserves, packets of pre-stamped note cards. She stretched a liver-spotted finger out and touched the care-worn hands of the farmers' spouses one after another, occasionally reaching to adjust her cardigan, to wrap it more closely around her frail shoulders. Her smile never faded. If there were two hundred families in town, at least half of them sent a representative to bid her farewell. I stood at her elbow, watching the church ladies pack her china and the local auctioneer appraise her furniture. They touched each item with reverence, as she had done.

That winter, we attended a pie supper for a family that had been burned out. Fire accounted for much loss in the country, since most people heated with wood and wood has a funny way of over-taking even the most diligent tending. I'm not much for baking but we brought an apple pie that my then-husband had made. It sold for three hundred dollars, the top take. The hippies of Murray Valley crowded in the community center shoulder to shoulder with the locals. Before the auction started, apron-clad wives ladled chili into Styrofoam bowls, with a hefty square of tender cornbread on the side. I hovered in the background, still a foreigner, in awe of the carefree disregard with which the women scrunched their faces in deep grins that furrowed the crow's feet beside their sparkling eyes. These women had earned their wrinkles, from fretting over crops, worrying about the building of barns, and wondering whether the old John Deere would last through harvest.

I shared breakfast this week with a friend, and something about the simple honesty of her countenance reminded me of one of the women of Murray Valley. All those years ago, when I sat at her kitchen table and complained about being an outsider, Jeanne turned her head to one side and gazed at me for several moments before replying. You've just got to step into the breach, she advised. And trust that someone will catch you, she did not add. I dismissed her advice and never felt at home. I left less than a year later.

Now I wonder if I've ever understood what she meant. I wonder, too, on which side of the breach I stand. I have lived in Brookside for eighteen years and have watched my former classmate age just yards from my porch, and have never made a legitimate effort to engage her in conversation. I don't know Johanna's surname, or the name of the retirement community to which she relocated. I can't tell you what ailment took Lise out of commission and forced her husband to walk alone for several months. I only know that her once-blond and plentiful hair is now silver and sparse. I know that she used to pedal a bicycle with vigor and now creeps forward in heavy, clunky shoes.

I can't help but think that something has gone amiss. I've watched the world spin, the world which now wonders if the approaching asteroid will drive a 1700-foot hole into its surface. If that rock hit my home, and I disappeared into the resulting crater, would anyone bother stepping into the breach to lend me a hand? I heard a speaker from Mexico talking about *Dia de Los Muertos* earlier this week. In some random context, he mentioned that his favorite Beatles lyric contained the best advice he'd ever heard: "And in the end, the love you get is equal to the love you give."

As I watched last evening, my neighbor raised her hand and rested it on her husband's arm, I drew a long breath, and briefly closed my eyes. I marveled at the ease with which she reached across that small space between them. Just before they moved out of sight, she turned her head backward, just slightly, in my direction. She caught my gaze across the expanse of my yard, and then, with seeming deliberation, turned away, and the two of them disappeared into the gathering dusk.

Mugwumpishly tendered,


Corinne Corley

# Thursday, November 6, 2014

*Death of My Favorite Curmudgeon:*
*Special Edition of the Saturday Musings*

Good afternoon,

This is not Saturday. I realize that. It is Thursday. I had intended to write this and send it out on Saturday morning and if you get this on Saturday, know that the writing, editing, and crying consumed me for long enough to have this arrive in your inbox more or less on time. If you get it before Saturday and insist on waiting until Saturday to read it, you will be perfectly within your rights. I am not Douglas Adams; I do not misname my creations with deliberateness.

Most of you who are reading these Musings know that my father-in-law, Jabez Jackson MacLaughlin, died yesterday, 05 November 2014. I would like to share the story of my relationship with Jay by way of my own private but publicized eulogy for him. I plan to attend his service but Jay had an aversion to funeral proceedings which included family members popping up and down to moan over the departed. He found it tacky. However, he liked my blog, and often read it, so I think I am safe in telling this story, here, today, in my way.

I first met Jay in the summer of 2009 when his son, James, and I started dating. Jay shocked me with his irascible nature and the somewhat dated views which he held and freely expressed. But he made a killer flan and always served

197

a special, non-red-meat entree for me when Jim and I came to his house for dinner.

In the early years of my relationship with Jim, I struggled to get my footing with his father. I once had a complete and total meltdown in his kitchen when he scolded me for stirring caramel and causing it to crystallize. His daughter, Virginia, placed her hand on my arm and counseled me to *Shake it off.* But shaking off the scoldings of the men in the generation above me does not come easily to me. It's no secret that my father, rest his soul, ruled our house with a leather belt, an abusive manner, and a volume level that would scare the paint off an old stairwell. Though I got the least of his wrath, being sickly and something of his favorite, still, I suffered enough of it and heard it all. I came to middle-age with a tendency to shiver and retreat when faced with an angry man.

Over the next three years, Jay and I fenced our way to an ability to tolerate, if not like each other. And then, as fate sometimes dictates, something arose to bind us inexorably to one another. His beloved wife Joanna became ill, and Jay and I, along with his children, became her care-givers. In the seven months between the onset of her last illness and her death, Jay and I became fast friends. I grew to love him, to listen to him, and to respect him. Over that year, I found a new way of understanding Jay. He never raised his voice to me though we did not always agree with one another. He treated me in that "old-fashioned" way that men of his era treat women, and as time passed, I no longer saw his proclivity to pay my way and hold doors for me as a sign that he thought me less significant due to my gender. In fact, it meant quite the opposite, and I learned that from him.

Jay received his diagnosis of cancer in June of this year. I found this development unsurprising. Joanna died on 08 October 2013 and he longed for her presence with an intensity that rendered me breathless. I felt he wanted to go to her, as she was clearly unable to return to him at least in any largely satisfying sense. And so, when he took me to lunch and talk-

ed about his cancer, and his inclination not to undergo chemotherapy, I reached the conclusion that he had no objection
to death even if he hoped not to suffer in the dying.

Still, speaking strictly for myself, I did not want to lose
my favorite curmudgeon. I loved him. I looked to him as a
father and felt honored that Jim and Virginia willingly tolerat-
ed my doing so. We had lunch and dinner outings, explored
the Internet, and had our own personal happy hours. He
called me several times a day in the year after his wife died.
He would call to check on me, to talk about a future dinner
date, to share some idea that he did not want to forget, or just
to hear my voice. By the end of his life, he had taken to calling
me sometimes six or more times each day and I would stop
nearly any pursuit (as long as there was not a judge involved)
to take his calls.

As the fall progressed, I found myself increasingly fearful that he would let himself slip away long before the year
that he had been given. I found myself bargaining with him
to prolong his life. The biggest pay-off would be the running
of the 90-day exclusion period for his Long Term Disability
policy. Jay liked nothing so much as the thought of sticking
it to that company and the mere mention of that potential
caused him to salivate. *Oh yes,* he would say. *Got to get my
money's worth for that policy.* I'd cast my nervous eye on him
and wonder if he meant what he said. He held his body in
a still, silent way which suggested otherwise. But I chose to
believe him. I had no recourse: To concede his impending
demise would cause me to lose my composure, and Jay hated
to see me cry.

By September, no one believed Jay should continue to
live at home alone, so off to a respite center for evaluation
he went. On one of his five nights there, I brought a fancy
Happy Hour kit, assembled by a clerk at the Plaza's Better
Cheddar. Jay loved Happy Hour. *It's five o'clock,* he would
say; and any whose attendance had been summoned had better be present or the drinks would be poured in their absence
and weak upon arrival.

I brought smoked salmon, and slices of expensive hard salami; fat ripe blackberries; good crackers; and a bottle of wine. His cousin Anne Jones arrived with her service dog, Katie, and a box of chocolates. We laid out the spread on the hospital bedside table and Jay ate the entire package of salmon and most of the salami. He drank the whole bottle of wine himself, save the half-inch that he allocated to me, allowing me to pretend that I drink without actually having to do so. Anne Jones called Katie to hop on the bed and Jay placed one spotted, worn hand on her head and smiled, with absolute tenderness.

Jay moved into assisted living at Brighton Gardens at the end of that week. We talked. He told me that he wanted to die at home and hoped that he could do so. He planned to use the sojourn in BG to "get strong" and move back to the house that he and Joanna had shared for nearly two decades. I indulged that dream. As far as I was concerned, I would fetch him back to his house in my car and stay 24/7 if that would give him an easy death.

But his decline continued. I'd tell him, *You can't die yet, Jay; we've got 60 more days til we can stick it to the insurance company,* and he'd reply, *Don't worry about that! I'm getting their money!*

In mid-October, I asked Jay if anyone had arranged for him to vote.

Now, the mere inquiry should cause your eyebrows to shoot skyward. I am by way of being a yellow-dog Democrat, Missouri-born and bred, daughter of a union organizer. I've actually been accused of being a Socialist, and but for the sheer unworkability of the philosophy, I find it appealing. Jabez J. MacLaughlin, on the other hand, was a life-long Republican who crossed party lines once to his deep regret and would never do so again. He broadcast that fact publicly and firmly, even vehemently, though never disrespectfully at least not in conversation with me.

But Jay was my father-in-law and I loved him dearly. I knew that he had taken a strong dislike to the candidate running against Senator Pat Roberts in Kansas; and that he scorned the process by which he believed the race came to be narrowed to two, with the withdrawal of the weak Democrat candidate for pretensive reasons and the resultant strengthening of the chances of the Independent.

So I told him that I would handle his application for an absentee ballot, but on one condition: That he promised not to die before the election. You see, I saw the look of death begin to gather round his eyes a month before he passed, and I longed to stave off the certain surrender as long as possible, because I am both greedy and shameless. I did not want to lose him.

I don't think Jay's zest for life prompted his to promise to live until November 4th. He yearned to be with Joanna, whom he knew waited for him. I often visited her resting place and told him of my visits, showing him pictures of the flowers which I brought. *Tell her that I will see her soon,* he'd instruct me. And I did. Every time.

No, Jay strove to endure because he wanted to vote against Senator Roberts' opponent by voting for Roberts.

I filed his application and the election board mailed the ballot. But it didn't come. On October 23rd, at my request, they mailed a second one. It still didn't come.

On the morning of Monday, November 3rd, Jay called me. We had discussed his voting in each of my visits the prior week, and I assured him that he would vote if I had to put him on a stretcher and push him to his polling place. But he grew weaker and I feared that voting in person would be hopeless. Had we thought, we could have changed his address to the facility, but that might have hastened his demise by destroying the charade which he liked to maintain that he would return home one day to die in his own bed. So the absentee ballot looked like the only option, with the potential for its receipt dwindling.

In that Monday morning call, Jay said, in a craggy voice which showed the gathering weakness, *I don't suppose there's much chance of my voting now, is there, honey? I'm getting weaker.* My heart clenched and my stomach turned but I kept that out of my voice and said: *I will get you a ballot if I have to walk to Olathe myself and bully someone into giving it to me. So hold on, Jabez J. MacLaughlin. You promised me.* And my favorite curmudgeon replied: *I'll try, honey; but hurry.*

I placed a call to Olathe and talked to my contact there. She passed me to a supervisor who passed me to someone else. I explained what had happened and Jay's situation and she said that I should come ahead and she would get things started. I got on the highway, weak eyes and all, and drove like the wind, following the directions which the lady had given me. I arrived at the Election Board and discovered a line of early voters which extended the length of the building. I told one of them why I was there and the line parted. Like Moses, I crossed the Red Sea.

At the counter, I told the woman that I needed to speak with Cheryl. She instantly replied, *Are you the lady with the dying father-in-law?* and I burst into tears held back since Westport. I did not need to answer.

Twenty minutes later, I had been certified as Jay's Election Assistant and slid back behind the wheel of my car, sparing only a few moments to fear getting stopped for my long-expired plates. I leaned my head on the steering wheel and remembered my mother's death in 1985 when, with expired plates, I drove from my cousin Theresa's house to my parents' house at 7:00 a.m. to see my mother's dead body, passing a police officer going 50 in a 35 with four months' gone tags. He stopped me but gave me a warning when I told him the nature of my errand. I prayed for such leniency on I-435 and took off.

At my father-in-law's bedside, I completed the forms for his voting process: my pledge, his designation of me, a copy of his driver's license. Then we started the ballot completion, with Jay too weak to fill in the black circles and me, the Democrat from St. Louis, doing it for him. With my help, he voted for Mr. Roberts and a score of other Republicans, and cast a vote against a couple of taxes and a judge with liberal tendencies which he described in a spat-out sentence which I will not here repeat. I take some credit for reminding him of that judge being on the ballot, for he had already said, in a fading voice, that he did not know or care about any of the judges.

Jay took the pen in his hand to sign his name to the ballot, and I steadied both page and pen. And when he had done, he laid back against his pillows and told me: *When Senator Roberts wins by one vote, I want you to call him and tell him that it was my vote, and that I voted for him in spite of himself.* And then he closed his eyes, his meager allotment of energy for the day spent.

I took the ballot to Olathe and returned to his room. I spent several more hours with him, just he and I. And the next day, Election Day, I abandoned my Democratic Party Certified Poll Challenger duties after only two hours to go and sit by his side until his son could arrive. He held my hand. He told me that he knew I loved him. I laid my head on his arm and wept; and he told me not to cry. He hated it when I cried.

By 1:30 on Tuesday, November 4th, 2014, Jay had slipped into a kind of sleep from which he would not emerge. His son and I sat by his bedside for that day and through the night. I kept my hand on his heart while he slept. And once again, the irony rose thick and full: I watched the election returns with Jim on Fox News, and injected my voice with enthusiasm as I kept my favorite curmudgeon apprised of the results. And when the tables turned, and the senate went red, I took his hand in mine and told him, *You did it, Jay; Senator Roberts won; and your party has taken the Senate.* And he smiled at me. I swear on my mother's grave: The news of the election results drew a smile from my favorite curmudgeon, as he lay in a sleep that would carry him to his Joanna's arms.

Forty-eight hours nearly to the moment from when he performed his last act, signing his name to that ballot, Jabez Jackson MacLaughlin slipped from us. His wife's love filled the room. One of his children held each hand. His death came easy. The deaths of good people should always be easy.

This morning, I crafted a letter to Pat Roberts. I told him a sanitized version of Jay's voting for him -- I pulled no punches about how Jay felt about him but left out the bits about my tears. I gave him Jay's message, and one of my own. I charged him with the responsibility of making Jay's endurance worthwhile. I asked him to do his duty, in honor to those who entrusted it to him,including and most especially my favorite curmudgeon..

Jay gave me something that I thought I would never have. He gave me the relationship of a father to a daughter. He loved me. He cherished me. He taught me, by example and by word; by action and by the smallest most meaningful gestures: the slight wave of his hand; the tilt of his eyes; the set of his jaw. That his son married me and gave me the most precious gift of being Jay's daughter-in-law endears him to me far beyond any love that I feel for my husband, far beyond any strain that our marriage has had, far beyond the cracks which might never be repaired. On the night that Jay died, I said that my words about Jay were mixed with the salt of a thousand unshed tears. And so they are: and so they shall stay, when the tears have fallen and dried; when the handkerchiefs have been re-washed; when the calendar's pages have fallen and withered.

When I go to visit them in their resting place --- Jabez and his Joanna -- I will place the roses on their headstones, and I will touch, briefly, their names engraved in the stone. And I will know, as surely as I know the enduring nature of their love, that I will never feel anything but gratitude for my curmudgeon and his beautiful bride. At the same time, though, I will never overcome the hole in my life where Jay once was, beside the hole that was once Joanna. A gossamer sheen might sweep itself over the rending. I can hope for little else.

But I will hold my head at the tilt which he taught me: Chin up; eyes bright; and smiling. For my tears hurt him; and he has suffered enough. His was a noble life though in many senses, a humble one. He raised two children and provided for them in a confident manner. He spent the last twenty years of his life traveling, and cooking, and caring for his Joanna. And me. He cared for me. Any goodness that still blooms in me, abides in part because of his tender nurturing of my spirit. And so, I bid farewell to my favorite curmudgeon. I will miss you. We never got to Lourdes, as we planned; but by God, we voted. We voted. And that's something of which we can both be proud.

Mugwumpishy tendered,

Corinne Corley

# Saturday Musings, 06 November 2010

Good morning,

The leaves gather beneath the holly bushes on which the first blush of winter berries has begun to gleam. I wrap myself in my usual ragtag selection of long scarves. I wind wool over chiffon and sweep the lot behind me as I descend the three steps of the porch, in the crisp air of the clear morning, with my usual cup of black courage clutched against my chest.

Last night, at another First Friday in Mission, a fine photographer and I joined forces to create a landscape for those gathered to view his works, and the works of the incomparable Katie Dallam, and the sweet paintings of a little girl with an eye for beauty. We arranged chairs, put out food, and made lemonade.

As we poured bottled spring water into the lemonade dispenser, I found myself thinking of other water, flowing from a spring, fed by an underground river, far south of here, in another lifetime.

In the mountains of Arkansas, a man with too much money built a house inside of a cave; not a hovel, nor a crude shelter, but a true house, with floors, and carpets, and a loft library, and bedrooms deep in the bowels of the old, craggy hillside, along a curved tiled hallway. The ceiling rose high, and the inner stairway ascended to a series of upper rooms, flanked by railings of carved wood tenderly made by crafts-men who knew their art.

The first time I drove the state highway to the cave house, we stopped beside the road to fill our thermos with water trickling from a pipe protruding out of the rough sweep of rock through which the road had been carved. I had never tasted water in its unsullied form. I had not known that water has a natural taste, and its own fragrance, and an unmistak-able light, as it moves within the earth.

The spring flowed with the unbridled force of its own energy, out of the small length of lead, unfettered, onto my hands, into my mouth as I bent over to drink. Not before or since has water given me what that water did: pure rejuvena-tion, as only things untainted by the processes we impose on them can give.

When we had consumed our fill, and capped our con-tainers, we continued on, and after a few minutes' drive along the road, we came around a broad bend and saw the cave house: windows where no windows should be, above a clear-ing that did not exist before wealth insisted on its creation, beside which sat an abandoned Bobcat. We parked alongside a battered pick-up and a BMW that must have belonged to the owner, for its paint gleamed, and its tires bore none of the mountain mud that vehicles can never shed once they be-came country cars.

We entered the cave house through a large wooden door of gleaming oak polished to an unnatural gloss and outfitted with heavy brass fittings. Inside we paused, staring, mesmer-ized by our surroundings. I raised my eyes and gazed upward, to the ceiling at the front part of the cave, towering fifty feet or more above me. To my left stood the stairway to the loft; its railing had not yet been installed, but the risers spanned four feet wide; to my right, I saw the hallway which curved away from us along the perimeter of the cave.

As my eyes adjusted to the light, I realized that I stood on natural stone, which, I was told, would ultimately be finished with wide planks of native wood flooring. We hovered near the doorway. I pulled my jacket closer to my frame. The air beneath the mountain would need no air conditioning.

After a few minutes, I became aware of a consistent, unfamiliar high-pitched sound. I asked, *What is that noise?* Came the reply from my companion: *Water. Water.*

My eyes finally adapted to the dimness of the interior, and I realized that in the great space that would someday be the grand foyer of the cave house, scores of buckets had been placed. Water dripped into those buckets, and onto the stone on which we walked with careful steps. The unbroken sound that it made as it fell signified that the mountain had not yet been tamed.

We toured the work-in-progress in silence, moving slowly, taking care on the slick, damp surface. We traversed the circular hallway, to the last point at which the workers had left their mark and then, with no backwards glance, slipped through a tall, narrow crevice into the bowels of the mountain.

I held my companion's hand and sometimes reached for the cool wall to steady myself in the passageway. We had no light other than weak rays from high above us. The silence only yielded to the sounds of the ubiquitous water and our own ragged respiration.

A hundred yards beyond the first opening, we came to another, smaller crack, and without hesitation, we sidled through it. I closed my eyes and clutched my companion's hand more tightly, as we moved deeper and farther beyond any place that humans often entered.

*Don't worry,* he said. *I know where I'm going.*

My breathing grew more desperate, and I felt the panic of the truly claustrophobic rise within me. At that point, turning back posed just as much terror as going forward, and so I kept walking, staggering blindly on the dark path until, suddenly, unexpectedly, the narrow passage opened into a wide expanse, the height of which soared to a place I could not see.

We stopped, my companion and I, and leaned against the rock wall, feeling its eternal cold press into our backs. As my body calmed, and I grew quiet, I realized that we stood on the shores of an underground lake, on the surface of which shone a snippet of light from somewhere so far above us that I had to take the naturalness of its source on faith. We held ourselves still, beside that pool, and we breathed air that few had ever breathed, that few even knew existed to be breathed.

We did not speak.

My fingers opened, and I realized that I had been grasping my companion's hand so tightly that my own hand ached.

*What is this place?* I whispered. I could not see his face.

*It is the heart of the mountain,* came his low reply.

Neither of us said anything more. I had no use for my eyes in the moment, and so I closed them, and I attended to the touch of virgin air on my skin and the quiet throb of unbroken silence. Gradually, the chill overtook us, and we joined hands once more.

At the far edge of the water, we slipped through another crack, into the space formed by the shifting of two large segments of rock, long ago, when the earth shuddered and shook. The steady dripping of water along the walls on either side of us and over our heads grew louder as we journeyed.

A hundred feet beyond the lake, the path began to rise, and my breathing grew labored from effort. My companion held onto me, wordlessly urging me forward as I struggled to climb. Finally, when I began to fear that I would have to surrender, and stay, living within the mountain like a troll, we broke through to the surface, and I gasped as I realized that once more we stood beside the spring at which we had so recently refreshed ourselves.

My companion led me to a flat rock, and I sank to its surface, eagerly lifting my face to the kiss of the summer sun. I could only silently nod as he told me that he would fetch the car. By the time he returned, I had fallen asleep, and I did not fully awaken as he guided me to the passenger's seat.

I visited the cave house many times after that, watching the workers press the trappings of civilization onto the mountain's stark interior. Gleaming, man-made surfaces formed under the rough, steady hands of silent locals who barely hid the contempt they felt. Whether their contempt was for the man whose dreams fed their families or for themselves, I never did decide.

When the last carpeting had been laid, and the last polished appliance fitted into the kitchen, and the last leather book slipped onto the walnut shelves installed in the loft, I came once more, to see what they had created. I walked the length of the hallway, to the end, where we had gone that day. I stopped, stunned.

But I should have known. The crevice had been closed, with brick, and mortar, and a heavy coat of something shiny -- sealant, I suppose, still emitting an acrid smell. I reached out, and ran my fingers along the smooth, hard wall. I closed my eyes and felt my body sway, just slightly, as I pressed my hand against that awful barrier. I turned, finally, and left, and I have not gone back.

I think about that lake from time to time, when the trees in my yard glisten with soft autumn rain, and I stand on my porch under its cathedral ceiling. I close my eyes, and I breathe the damp, cool air, and I am transported, just briefly, back to that inner sanctuary, to the shore of the quiet, old lake, under the ancient mountain. And I remember the delicate taste of spring water, and its soothing touch, as it fell into my hands from a pipe staked in a rock, in Newton County, when I was young.

Mugwumpishly tendered,


Corinne Corley

# Saturday Musings, 10 November 2012

Good morning,

Another trial crashed against a cliff of stone, the rising jagged bluff of justice that stands on the western side of the state. Thirty days to draft proposed findings and the rest of the night following yesterday's conclusion to rethink each decision, each strategic choice, the potential rise or fall of my client's prospects eternally tied to the wager he made in retaining me and the thousands of dollars he spent in the year since he did so. Another sleepless night.

I rose this morning an hour later than my usual Saturday, two hours after the standard time on my alarm for the last month. I drank my morning coffee on the porch, pleasantly half-shaded from the sun's sweet rays, surrounded by the swirl of leaves from the neighbor's tall, aging oak. Pages of the morning paper drifted under my tired eyes, half-veiled by the shimmer of white that the eye doctor says will eventually recede as my brain adjusts to its presence. The absence of political rhetoric in the pages of the Star both delights and confounds me: *Where is the news?* I find myself thinking, but all I am given is paragraph after paragraph of the accidents, robberies, plays, and street improvements around my town. Another election forgotten; another turn of history's wheel, another inch closer to eternity.

As I draw in the fresh air outside, I feel the sweetness of every November, the unpredictable weather that Missourians smugly claim as their particular province. I feel again the gentle chill of Novembers of my childhood: Thanksgivings spent huddled in wool sweaters, deliciously shivering on my parents' front porch while my brothers played football in the front yard. I hear my mother's voice singing in the kitchen, she standing at the window over the sink, watching the sway of the neighbor's tree. She would turn to smile as I kneaded the dough from which our Thanksgiving clover-leaf rolls would be made. She would place one worn, brown-spotted hand over my smaller, paler fingers, and push down, giving the dough what it should have without scolding me for doing it wrong. The warm fragrance of yeast rose around us, mingling with the fragrance of roasting turkey and the sweet tang of whole berries simmering on the stove.

My mother made the pies ahead of time, perhaps on Wednesday night. She seemed to know what pies had to be refrigerated and which ones could rest on the counter, knowledge that I never gleaned from her, a distinction that still confuses me. My father watched television in the living room while she cooked. I see my sisters in the kitchen with us, taller than me, moving around the small space between counter and stove, the creation of Thanksgiving dinner orchestrated like the best ballet. Three times each year we used my mother's good china: Easter, Thanksgiving and Christmas. The sterling came out from the bottom of the china cabinet on such holidays, the flatware and the napkin rings, the small plates from Grandmother Corley on which dessert would be served. We polished the silverware, simmering badly tarnished pieces in baking soda water on a burner set to low. The linen tablecloths had to be ironed, water sprinkled from an old dish washing liquid bottle in those days before steam irons. After the table cloth came the napkins themselves, one daughter ironing, one daughter folding, and I with my little girl hands sliding them into the rings, each one with an engraved name. Richard, Lucille, Ann, Adrienne, Joyce, Kevin, Mark, Mary, Francis, Stephen.

Every dish had to be completed at the precise moment when the dinner would be served, at the correct temperature. The cranberry sauce might have been made a day earlier, so that its tangy chill could set. The turkey came out to rest while the rolls baked and the casserole of that green bean stuff heated through and the marshmallows cut in half to adorn the yams melted and took on their golden glow. The older girls helped my mother put the dishes on the table, and someone raised the camera to photograph the feast. Then the boys were called to come into the house; while their clamoring rose, and the pounding of their feet hammered on the stairs, my father stood sharpening the knife at the kitchen counter. I hear the sharp whisk of steel against steel, each draw of the knife sending wicked shivers through my body.

The table in our breakfast room held ten. Its Formica expanse hidden beneath linen transformed the humble dining set. Each child took their assigned seats: for most of my childhood, I sat to the left of my father at the far end. My parents waited for our chattering to stop, and then we murmured the grace: *Bless us, Oh Lord, and these they gifts, which we are about to receive...* Then the first draw of the knife through the turkey's crisp skin sent the steamy fragrance heavenward, and the blessings became obvious indeed.

As the serving bowls went around the table, and butter got smeared on warm rolls straight from the oven, we said our Thankful-Fors. Each person, youngest to oldest, disclosed that for which they felt gratitude. The boys often opted for their special dish; the girls, something more sweet. My mother's thankful-for varied with the times: her job, the health of a child who had been particularly ill, or something more vague, a cryptic reference about which I do not believe I ever wondered: "prayers answered", and I never asked my mother, not once, what it was for which she had prayed.

In my memory, the Thanksgiving meal stands as the most special of each year. Easter's fragrant, yeast-dough-wrapped ham; the roast at Christmas; the backyard barbecue at the Fourth of July -- nothing compares to the richness of dressing roasted in the bird, fresh-whipped cream, and the first bite into the crisp brown exterior of gooey marshmallow over the brown-sugar glazed sweet potatoes. My childhood days held frightening turbulence, which coalesced as flinty memories that pierce my nights at times, recollections I should have let slip into the morass of age. But I remember nothing unpleasant about any Thanksgiving. I recall only the warmth of my mother's body standing behind me in the kitchen, guiding my hands; my father holding a heavy, china serving dish while he coaxed me to accept more food than he knew I would eat, my brothers clamoring to claim the turkey legs and the biggest ladle-full of thick, salty gravy.

The yammer of the Car Guys tells me that I've lingered too long at the keyboard. My coffee has completely cooled, forgotten on the gilt-edged plate that I use as a coaster on my little desk. I've raised the wood-slat blinds, and I can see the clearness of the day and the blueness of the sky, against the wintry leaves. The wind has risen, and the neighbor's patio umbrella tosses its green canvas as a small brown critter skitters on the surface of the table. I should be doing something constructive, like laundry, or Yoga, or cogitating on the likely outcome of this week's trial. Instead, I think that I will gather all of the books I have read in the last two weeks, and take them to the Mystery bookstore. I'll tender them for store credit, order an Americano from the coffee bar, and browse the shelves of international writers. By and by, I'll choose the next in a series of which I am fond, or maybe the first in a series that I haven't read. I'll take a chair in the far back of the reading room and lose myself in the pages of other people's lives.

Mugwumpishly tendered,


Corinne Corley

# Saturday Musings, 17 November 2012

Good morning,

The stretch down Truman Road between the Independence square and I-435 can be driven on auto-pilot. A day or
two ago, as I made that sweeping pass towards the highway
that would take me back to my office, the rambling tones of
Steve Kraske, a Kansas City Star reporter who interviews local celebrities on public radio, filled the chilly confines of my
car. A lilting laugh rose to meet his deeper, friendly chuckle.
Kraske asked Joyce DiDonato, the opera star who hails from
Prairie Village, Kansas, about her new recordings. I barely
attended to their chatter. I do not like opera.

But he switched gears: Another new release, this one
filled with more colloquial tunes. And I nearly drove the
Saturn into a curb as Ms. DiDonato's voice threw me back
to 1973 as she sang "When You Walk Through a Storm," the
Rogers and Hammerstein signature song of my high school
baccalaureate.

I stood again beneath an arching, raised roof amid painfully modern contours of Corpus Christi Church. The middle
section in the vast space held row on row of parents clad in
Sunday finery. They twisted to watch the back of the church,
where I and my classmates have submitted to being adorned
with the ragged petals of a giant, white chrysanthemum. We
each hold a single yellow rose. We've been aligned in our

customary alphabetical order, a few dozen eighteen-year-old girls whose fate awaits on the other side of the gloom. The notes of the organ start, and the first girl, the girl who has always been first by the coincidence of alphabet, steps forward.

With my surname, I found myself grouped in the first third of any line. I followed the swishing skirt of the girl ahead of me, pulled forward by the music, as the chorus repeated. Some one's mother, or a nun, or maybe a junior, sang the lyrics standing in front of a microphone at the far side of the nave. The size of our class, the last graduating class of the doomed high school, allowed us to finish the journey before the brave notes subsided. Our Baccalaureate Mass began. Fragrance rose around us, a curious, cloying mixture of mums, roses and burning candles. At some appropriate moment, each of us tendered the yellow flower to our mothers, long stems catching on our sleeves, thorns lightly scratching the tender skins of our hands.

To the communion rail, to our seats, down the aisle through the doors at the back of the church. The strains of the organ sent us on our way. A great noise arose, voices of my classmates, their laughter, their unbridled whoops of self-congratulation. The din of disorder overcame me. I pulled away. My eyes spanned the throng of exiting parents, searching for my own mother, who had sat in the church by herself, a bit away from the others, in a pale blue dress with frayed cuffs and collar, clutching a vinyl navy handbag.

I spied my mother's mottled brown countenance, the worn face broken only by a thin line of mauve lipstick, her plucked brows slightly drawn. I could not see her eyes behind the reflections on the lenses of her glasses. By the set of her jaw, and the arch of her chin, I knew she despaired of finding me. The voices of my classmates and their proud parents swelled and filled the vestibule. I stood apart, near the door, unable to force myself to advance towards her. A cluster of students in pretty frocks flanked by their mothers and fathers barred my mother's way. Thus did we hover, a world apart, separated by something more dire than a mere gaggle of girls.

216

Just before my mother surrendered to defeat, just before the moment when she might have turned and left the building by another exit, an avenue opened in the chattering crowd, and she saw me, standing alone, watching her.

Our eyes met. Her hand fell, slowly, to her side, the petals of the rose I had given her brushing the wrinkled skirt of her dress. I cannot know what she thought, in that moment. I cannot know if she understood what held me back. I cannot say whether the treachery rising in my heart had reached my face.

She stepped towards me before I could summon myself to move. But I met her halfway. In the center of the crowd of exuberant graduates, my mother and I embraced.

The strains of Joyce DiDonato's beautiful rendition of the Rogers & Hammerstein classic died away as I made the final swoop onto the highway. I shook off the bittersweet memories of the past, and signaled my lane change. By the time I got to my office, only the lovely hopefulness of the song lingered in my mind, entwined with the memory of the widening smile on my mother's face, just before I took her in my arms.

Mugwumpishly tendered,


Corinne Corley

# Saturday Musings, 24 November 2012

Good morning,

The sun shines higher than usual as I sit at my old writing desk, my computer slightly listing when the wobbly legs occasionally shift. I hear mild coughing from a downstairs bedroom, signaling that one of the sentient beings in the house stirs. I've slept later because the demands of the last few weeks have taken a terrible toll on my aging bones. With a little pharmaceutical boost, I managed to reclaim some needed rest.

The annual food fest on which we gorge ourselves and then spend too much on material goods of dubious quality passed with muted fanfare this week. I cooked a passable turkey, less monstrous than normal but still tasty rolls, that ubiquitous green bean casserole, and dubious bread pudding, all of which we hauled to my in-laws' house. The service and grace seemed strange to me but apparently comported with the traditions of my husband and his family-of-birth, so I smiled and silently relinquished my own preferences. But tonight the friends who normally gather at my table this time of year will do so again, and there will be a round of "thankful-fors", and the serving dishes will pile up on the table, and I will have the best of both worlds.

The only shopping I did this Black Friday involved a stolen moment at Prospero's, a used bookstore which recently opened a new location near my office, and a couple of stops to find shoes with my visiting son. The latter journey took place within the small, clean confines of the Kia that Patrick just purchased from our neighbor, with the CD emitting strains of his favorite music and he behind the wheel. Either his driving has improved or my backseat driving has diminished. I found myself relaxing as a passenger for the first time since he got his license five or so years ago. I even liked some of the songs on the mix CD he played. Some. Not all -- but some.

I don't need to close my eyes to see my mother standing in the doorway of our living room, surrounded by the blaring notes of Joe Cocker, or Frank Zappa, or maybe Jerry Garcia, coming from the long, low stereo she had purchased with the proceeds of many weeks of saving S&H Green Stamps. My brothers sit on the floor, on the thin grey carpet, and I re-cline in a yellow wing-back chair with worn arms. I cannot imagine that I am older than twelve or thirteen; my brother Kevin is four years older than I am, and left home straight away after high school. So we are teenagers, on this afternoon in my memory, probably on break from school, Thanksgiving perhaps, with the steely sky outside our windows.

*I was sitting in the breakfast room trying to balance my checkbook and pay bills,* my mother says. *And as I gritted my teeth, striving to concentrate despite the blaring of this -- do you call it music? -- I told myself, "Oh, Lucy, it's not so bad. They could be out robbing banks."* My mother pauses, laughs, shrugs her shoulders. *And then I looked at my bank balance and I thought, What's wrong with them?! They could be out robbing banks!!!*

One of the boys turns the volume down a notch, and another rises from the floor and crosses to where my mother stands. They had both surpassed her height by then, and she looks up to the face of whichever one has come to cajole her back to good humor. He takes her hand and pulls her into the open area in front of the couch and twirls her around, a waltz timed to the hard beat of rock and roll. He dips and spins her small frame, and as she dances, her skirt swirls around her sturdy legs. It is a denim wrap-around skirt, one of a dozen she made from the same pattern in different fabrics. Soon, they are all three dancing, my brothers and my mother, while I sit in my mother's favorite chair singing along with the stereo.

Someone recently asked me if I had a happy childhood. I could not answer the question. I had a strange childhood, with peaks and valleys. I traveled through childhood strapped in the middle car on a crazily high roller coaster, plunged to terrifying depths and thrown to exhilarating heights. If my life had a soundtrack, it would include tracks by Dvorak, Livingston Taylor, Willie Nelson, and always, the Grateful Dead. The liner notes would pay special attention to those who taught me cruel lessons as well as those who gave me safe harbor from the ravaging of the winter winds. And to the loss of those in the forward cars: "Fare thee well, Fare thee well, I love you more than words can tell."

I tried to give my son less for which to be grateful in the starkness of its lessons, and more to appreciate for the sweetness of its scenery. I do not know if I was successful. He stomps in and out of the house as though either driven by demons of his own or propelled by a fantastic ambition which he can barely contain. Or both, maybe. His writing shocks and astonishes me with its deft combination of irony and joy, its overtones of presumed defeat tempered with abiding hope. *But it's okay,* I tell myself. *He could be out robbing banks.*

I am thankful that he is not. And there is so much for which I feel gratitude, including, I must admit, the heart-wrenching memory of my mother dancing with my brothers, to the pounding rhythms of "Casey Jones."

Mugwumpishly tendered,


Corinne Corley

# Saturday Musings, 10 December 2011

Good morning,

I've balanced my laptop on a wooden table purchased at an estate sale for five dollars, more years ago than I can recall. A stout cup of French roast cools at my elbow. At the far end of the scarred oak dining table, an assemblage of Christmas decorations stands at the ready for a later event.

The five-foot tree purchased a decade ago at a January half-price sale shines in its customary corner, lights glowing, only a few plastic needles falling to the floor. Christmas stands proud at the end of the next two rows of boxes on my German calendar. I braved the "early shoppers" sale at Kohl's yesterday, and even did a round at Target, being as I needed cat food any way. Every single sales clerk whom I encountered flashed smiles; but then, it's early yet.

Nearly sixty Christmases span the backward circuit of my life. As I make my lists, check them twice, buying presents for everyone regardless of whether I consider them naughty, or nice, I think about successful purchases in the past: the radiant smile of my best friend's granddaughter Nora just last year, when she opened a life-size, soft Christmas doll; my son's grin at the remembered request of a clock made from reclaimed computer parts, which he had spied at the VALA Gallery; and years ago, the same boy's shrieks upon spying the tall Batman with light-up eyes that Santa had finally found after searching a dozen stores.

But one of the most satisfying presents that I've purchased -- and I have purchased hundreds -- was the American/French idiomatic dictionary that I bought for my cousin Kati's then-husband Bernard in 1983.

He had little English at the time. Kati and I had reunited on their relocation from St. Louis to Kansas City, sitting for hours in their apartment chattering about our childhood and the decade of events since our college days. Bernard could not follow our conversation. He thumbed through a French-English dictionary and could not determine the meanings of phrases rushing around him in our common St. Louis twang.

For weeks, he grumbled about his crazy American wife and her wild cousin Corinne, though said in French it sounded elegant. I got it into my head that he might feel less alienated if he understood our vernacular, so I set about -- in the days before Al Gore invented the World Wide Web -- to find a French/American idiomatic dictionary.

Not easy, I discovered.

My search extended to the considerable reach of area bookstores available at the time. Harried clerk after harried clerk shook head after tired head. Finally, in Whistler's Books, then located in Westport, a salesman took pity on me. *I'll try,* he said, in a weary voice, seven staggering shopping days before Christmas. *Don't get false hopes,* he cautioned, and turned away to answer a question about the tells-all-star-biography-of-the-week, which *No, we do not carry, we are an independent bookseller, we don't carry that kind of stuff, try Walden Books,* he said, with only a slightly disdainful sneer.

Kati and Bernard had invited me to share a meal at their home for the holiday. I could never have declined. In addition to my craving for the company of family, the allure included the fact that Bernard, a French chef, would certainly provide something succulent and decadent. But I did not want to go without a present for Bernard, and I had despaired of finding what I wanted most to give him. I purchased a back-up -- I think it was a boring wool scarf -- and hoped it would suffice.

A half hour before I should have been arriving at their apartment, the phone rang. *You ordered a book from us,* said a very, very tired voice. *It's here.* I drove faster than I should through the thick traffic of last-minute shoppers, not noticing the lovely rise of Christmas lights on the Plaza, narrowly escaping a crash with Cinderella's horse-drawn carriage in my haste to get to Whistler's Books before it closed. My parking karma provided a narrow spot into which I crammed my vehicle, and I slammed the car door, barely pausing to lock it, arriving ten minutes before the store closed, and fifteen minutes after my scheduled arrival time at Kati and Bernard's apartment.

The man who had called was the same man who had promised to try to find the book. He handed it to me, and I gazed down at it with surprise. Slightly battered, a little careworn, clearly used, nonetheless, it bore the title: Dictionary of American to French Idiomatic Translations. Or something like that. I looked at the clerk. *How did you find it,* I asked, with true wonder.

He smiled. *I searched a lot of catalogs at first,* he told me. *Books in Print, too. Then, when nothing I did worked, I called a friend of mine.*

The friend, it turned out, ran a bookstore in New York City. That friend had a friend who ran a bookstore in Paris, France. That friend had a friend who ran a used book stall on a side street in Paris, a hand-made structure with a slanted tin roof that did not even have a name. In the stall stood a small shelf of guides for French folks planning to travel in various countries, and on that shelf, my present for Bernard had waited. The Paris bookseller bought it, shipped it to the New York book store owner, who sent it to Kansas City, where I purchased it for less than the postage to mail it from France.

I gazed at the salesman with frank admiration. *So much trouble for one book,* I murmured, running my hands along its cracked spine. He shrugged. *I told them about your cousin's husband,* he admitted. *About the two of you talking all night in their living room, and poor Bernard sitting in the kitchen, clueless as to what half your chattering meant. We all felt bad for the poor guy.* He shrugged again, a careless lift of a wool-clad shoulder. I got the sense that his efforts rose more from his sympathy for a man with a crazy wife, and a crazy cousin-in-law, than from his desire to satisfy a customer. The motivations of the New York and Paris connections, I can only imagine.

I wished him a *very Merry Christmas.* I left the store, unwrapped book clutched to my chest, and made my way to Kati and Bernard's apartment. The meal did not disappoint, nor did the shining smile on Bernard's face when he saw his gift.

In an hour, three seven-year old girls will descend upon my home, to decorate my Christmas tree and paint glass ornaments. One of them, my friend Elisabeth's daughter Accalia, has hired herself out for the morning to raise money for Operation Smile (www.operationsmile.org). I will compensate her efforts with a check to that charity. I invited the others -- my friend Sherri's nieces, Courtney and Allie -- just to make a merry morning. I will feed them ants-on-a-log, and take their pictures to post on Facebook. When they have gone, I will sit in my rocker by the fireplace, and gaze upon the ornaments dangling from the branches of my artificial tree, recalling each Christmas that I have spent in this home. When I start to feel that I have been lazy enough, I will set aside that pleasant occupation, and get on with my day.

Mugwumpishly tendered,


Corinne Corley

# Saturday Musings, 15 December 2012

Good morning,

Ten days remain between us and December 25th; and as the steam rises from my coffee cup, I think of what I have left to accomplish. Three hearings, perhaps a fourth judging by a message left on Friday by a desperate prospective client; a half-dozen presents to buy; the tree to finish decorating; and meals to cook, including finding a recipe for palatable gluten-free cookies. In between those tasks, there are clients to harass for payment so that I can afford all those presents; and year-end taxes to turn my salon-colored hair grey; and one or two outstanding judgments to draft.

And as I raise the mug to take another sip, internally grumbling, my eyes chance to fall on today's banner headline, and the fretting falls away, leaving only a well of gratitude. One word spans the columns, in three-inch type: *Horrific.*

When our suite-mate rushed into the office to tell us about the massacre in Connecticut, my stomach lurched. *Dear God, not more children killed,* but my prayer came too late. And as I sat in front of my computer screen, a wellspring of conflicting emotions flooded my chest: *Those poor babies; that monster; how are the parents going to struggle through this?*

And one other thought rose unbidden, a kind of emotional deja vu, which sent my heart's call to the children huddled under those desks: *How terrified they must have been.* And I sank back, back, back two decades, to the path I trod down a hall of Kansas University Hospital, behind a rapidly striding doctor. A path of which I might have spoken here before today, but one that repeats so often in my mind, so rarely described, that I see now, I should take others down that path with me, so that one kernel of truth might be exposed.

A friend had taken me to KU because I felt pains in my "right lower quadrant" and my temperature had elevated. Neither of us knew with certainty what the signs of appendicitis might be. We each had memories of rudimentary instructions in first aid class, and the pain combined with the fever seemed to suggest trouble. So off we went, two recent transplants to Kansas City, to the closest hospital.

An overworked resident suggested that I might have hours to wait before lab results confirmed or dispelled our worries. I decided to go out into the waiting room and release my friend. No cell phones in 1981, but I assumed that a nurse would let me call my friend to come get me when they decided I could go home. So I pulled my jeans onto my skinny legs, exited the exam room clutching the hospital gown closed, and turned right.

The emergency room corridors formed an inner square with the exam rooms on the outer perimeter and the nurses' station sitting squarely in the middle. I could not know that precisely at the moment when I acted from concern that Joyce would spend the entire night slumped in an uncomfortable chair watching reruns of old sitcoms, Bradley R. Boan entered the emergency room armed with a shotgun and a bad disposition. He then lurched forward a few steps, into the very corridor which I traversed. Between him and me, Dr. Marc Beck strode, long-limbed and intent, chart in hand, probably not even watching ahead of him, oblivious to the fact that there would be no more Christmases, no more patients, no more life.

When the shotgun blast sounded, I dove down an intersecting corridor and ran towards what I believed to be the exit. I had chosen badly: I found only an abandoned waiting room, chairs strewn with jackets, coats, and magazines. I stood against the wall, frantic, listening to the screams, the shoving of furniture, the hurrying into rooms, the barring of doors. A second blast, as Boan dispatched with a patient's mother sitting in a wheelchair to the right of the entrance, savagely and senselessly,

And then: an eerie silence, punctuated only by the occasional ringing of an unattended phone.

I gazed in front of me, at my own grim face reflected in a darkened window. I realized that if I could see the reflection of the corridor in the window, anyone coming into the corridor could see me. I dove for the closest door, into an examining room, where I waited for what seemed an eternity, alone, under the examination table, the door blocked by a cart that I had shoved in front of it.

The evening progressed: eventually, all of us were herded into one room, and later, escorted to the dark parking structure in which KBI agents had shot light after light, hoping to flush out the suspect whom they thought was hiding there. As it happens, he had long since fled, and would not be captured until he unleashed his fury on another place of healing: a church. He would be caught, tried, and unsuccessfully attempt to blame mental illness. Conviction affirmed, film at ten.

As I sit in my dining room, 21 plus years later, the terrible tragedy in Connecticut raises the hairs on the back of my neck. Grief draws tears: grief for the children whose lives ended with the deadly accurate aim of a ruthless murderer. But grief also for the children huddled nearby under desks, in corners. Layer upon layer of pain will unfold in their minds, drawn forth as they mature, bubbles rising to the surface, or foaming beneath the cool plane of their passive faces. Time after time, they will ask themselves the question that lurks in the gloomy corners: *Why them? Why not me?*

Years after my brief encounter with a killer's rage, I stood in the bathroom at my home in Winslow, Arkansas. The drug store kit had shown a solid "plus", foretelling the birth of my son. Eyes met reflected eyes. The chill of winter surrounded me; the future loomed, with its sleepless nights, its momentary flashes of regret, its joys, its triumphs, its fears. As I stared into my own future, shining in the light of my reflected countenance, I felt the surge of survivor's guilt that I can never shake. So much has happened to me, so many things that others could not bear. A chaotic childhood. A few lost years, drowned in single malt. Some ravaged relationships, a few that left scars, some that left bruises that faded only in the corporal world. Shot at, run down, left for dead.

And yet, still living. Where others bled and died, I rose, a crippled Phoenix, with tattered feathers, and flew on, sometimes knocked off course, but still soaring. Why them? Why not me?

The coffee pot sounds three bells, telling me it has shut off. The crickets which sing in my inner ear raise their voices. The rest of the house stands silent. One glance tells me that the headline has not changed: 20 children still lay in the morgue, six adults to watch over them forever. In an hour or so, a friend will pull into my driveway, and we will go sit over brunch, warm food in our bellies, steaming tea in a pot, chasing away the cares of the week with the same sort of ease that a lunatic ended the lives of twenty-six innocents.

Mugwumpishly tendered,


Corinne Corley

# Saturday Musings, 24 December 2011

Good morning,

The stack of wrapped presents begins to grow on my dresser. Two carry bags on the floor hold additional gifts, sorted by the households to which they will be taken. A third pile has yet to be wrapped, and in my closet, more await. As I cut paper and pull tape, I try to cough away from my work, desperate to keep my germs to myself.

I lean against the bed, gazing at the happy results of my shopping efforts. Simply put, I love Christmas. I'm not religious but I have adopted this holiday as my opportunity to bestow each person in my world with a tangible manifestation of my gratitude for their existence.

Yesterday, my secretary opened the small gift that I had chosen for her while shaking her head back and forth. I thought I saw her hands tremble. She has worked for me for just a few months, and I know nothing of her life, nothing that would explain the emotion displayed as she lifted the scarf and truffles from their gift bag. As I left an hour or so later, she spoke in a faltering voice: *I'd sure like to give you a hug.* I put my arms around her thin frame. Merry Christmas, merry, merry Christmas.

I've purchased many scarves for people through the years. I give my friend Basimah a new scarf each Christmas and birthday. I'm not sure how she wears them all, but I am certain that she will never have to buy one for herself. I try to think of another gift to give her, but find myself standing in front of the display of silk, cashmere and wool, caressing the lovely threads, fascinated by the shimmering colors, choosing yet another piece of fabric that she can wind around her neck or drape over her shoulders. She has never said, *Enough, enough!* and accepts each with the same sweet, sincere smile.

Years ago, when I was a senior in high school, I purchased a matching hat, scarf and mitten set for a little girl whom I tutored. I used my babysitting money to buy them. I stood in Kresge's dime store for a long while, running my fingers over the knitted yarn. I imagined the child with her stringy, unwashed blond hair, and her deep blue eyes, and thought about the colors and how they would frame her face. I shifted from foot to foot, debating, and finally chose the red set, imagining the bright pom pom atop her small head, thinking of the light in her eyes as she tore away the paper and opened the box.

The following Saturday, I traveled to the church at 14th and Mallincrot in St. Louis for the Christmas party staged for our students by the parish sponsor of the tutoring program. I gazed out of the window of the vehicle in which my friends and I rode, watching the suburban houses fall away as we traveled south and east into the city proper. Apartment buildings with broken sidewalks took their place, and the quiet streets of our county neighborhood yielded to blaring horns and sirens; clean pavement gave way to littered slush.

But inside the church, dozens of small boys and girls chattered as volunteers handed out paper cups filled with hot chocolate. Among them, I found my student standing silent, gazing at the colored light bulbs draped from the folding table which held plates of cookies.

As the other children eagerly pulled toys from gift bags, my girl gently lifted the scarf and held it high enough to keep it from draping on the floor. I stood over her, encouraging her to wind it around her thin neck. I settled the beret around her curls and eased each of her tiny hands into a crimson mitten. She stood, gazing at me, wearing an expression that I could not understand, not moving, holding her thin frame rigid. I finally took pity on her, and removed the knitwear, returning it to the box. I thought she would run off then, but she reached for the gift and clutched it against her chest, and said, *thank you so much for these beautiful things,* and as she spoke, tears ran down her face.

The next week, my girl came to tutoring without her hat, or scarf, or mittens. When I asked about them, she shrugged. After the session, I mentioned them to our teacher, who told me that likely they had been lost or stolen. I felt a small measure of regret for having given her something so transient, something so briefly brightening her life.

At the end of the session, I learned that no one had come to retrieve my student, and that we would be delivering her to her parents' home. She sat beside me in the car without speaking, holding my hand, gazing out the window. When we parked near her building, she quickly wiggled out of the car and swiftly walked away from me, with only the briefest of glances in my direction. I stood beside the car, troubled, and from that vantage point, saw the door of the building open and her mother's narrow frame step onto the sidewalk.

The rush of shock propelled me forward several steps before my teacher's hand stopped me. We watched my student's mother walk forward to greet her, wearing a flimsy, tattered dress, a scarlet hat on her head, a matching scarf wound around her neck, and mittens on each hand. From the short distance between us, I could see hollow cheeks and dark smudges under sunken eyes. I saw the woman reach for her daughter with long, fragile arms, drawing her close, pulling her into the yawning gape of the battered door which closed behind them with a dreadful thud.

There was nothing to do but get back into the car and leave the place. The other girls talked happily among themselves during the ride home. When the car stopped, they spilled out onto the parking lot and called holiday wishes to each other as they ran to their parents' cars. I got out last, and stood waiting for my ride to arrive. The teacher spoke my name, and I met her eyes with a sharp snap of my head. *Merry Christmas,* she whispered, as my mother's Ford pulled into the driveway. I did not reply.

Decades later, my son's cell phone starts to ring and buzz in his bedroom. He's scheduled for his customary volunteer work with Meals on Wheels today. In a few minutes, he will stagger out and grunt a request for coffee. He will have tarried too late over his guitar and his computer. We finished Christmas shopping last evening, with dozens of other people at Barnes and Noble, where we had a coffee and talked about his fall trip to West Virginia: *We went out one night with a bunch of people that I didn't know, and I had a really good time. That trip was great,* he told me, and I believed him, for rarely do I see him speak with such uncontrived passion.

I purchased a scarf for my son this year, and as I wrapped it in tissue and gently placed it into a box last night, I thought about my little girl and her mother. I remembered the look in her eyes above the box which she clutched to her chest. I saw again the brief flash of red disappear behind a heavy door, and I felt again the cruel bite of wind on a St. Louis street, long ago, under a leaden sky.

Mugwumpishly tendered,


Corinne Corley

*Merry Christmas, and God Bless You, Each and Every One*

# Saturday Musings, 29 December 2012

Good morning,

An hour's worth of eloquence just went off to the land of accidentally deleted material, and I am loath to reconstruct it. I curse this technology. My old Mac has died; my son's Dell jumps to delete every time I hit the space key, and I drafted the Musings on my tablet. When I tried to copy the material, the entire thing deleted. While "Alt, C" meant "copy" on the Mac, it evidently means "cut" on the tablet. Pardon me, therefore, for the resulting brevity. The memories of Christmas and New Year's Eve once deftly here recorded now exist only in my brain. I swear, what I wrote shone with brilliance.

My little brother visited last night, with his son Deion, en route to St. Joseph where Deion is even now registering for a baseball showcase, at which a hundred small colleges, D2 and D3, will gaze on him and other high-schoolers, determining to which of them they might make overtures. Frank's call asking if they could stay with us came on the heels of my early New Year's resolution to repair my relationships with my siblings. That resolution, in turn, followed a quiet Christmas with my in-laws, partaking in their rituals, missing the rituals of my family of birth. My life turns another circle, my hair turns a little more grey, and the time of my reconciliation looms. I might be a bit belated in my efforts to mend the tears in my life's fabric, but I have taken up my needle, and some good, strong thread.

Frank and I toured my home, gazing on things that once belonged to my mother. We speculated on where each stood in our childhood home. He touched the blue pitcher with a large but gentle hand, and stood in front of the picture of Mary with the babe, surrounded by shepherds. *In the hallway?* he queried, and that jived with my memory. A red glass cornucopia rested on the top shelf of my mother's china cabinet. Dust now lies on each of the handful of pieces that I have from my mother's home. We only briefly mentioned the items stored in a brother's basement, which apparently vanished in a burglary. It's all gone; there's no need, no use, no reason to wonder where it really went.

As Frank and Deion backed out of our driveway, my son stood beside me, holding a cup of coffee. *I played lightsabers with that kid,* he recalled. *We used trash can lids for shields."* The cold drove us back into the house, where we washed dishes, and brewed another pot of coffee. Then my son decided to sleep for a few more hours, and I took my coffee upstairs, where I wrote my usual drivel, though slightly better, I'd like to think, now that it has been accidentally deleted.

On New Year's Eve, many decades ago, my brothers and sisters and I banged on Club aluminum pots with wooden spoons, calling to neighbors who stood on their own porches. Gunfire, honking horns, and fireworks rang through our neighborhood. When the commotion subsided, my mother beckoned us back into the house where hot cocoa and pastries awaited. We sat at the breakfast table, straining against sleep, making silly jokes to stay awake. Eventually, my mother chased us off to our rooms, and we snuggled under the covers, confident that when we awakened, the dawn of a fresh new year would offer hope for our heart's desire.

From my little desk, where the Saturday sun struggles through the heavy clouds and streams through my window, I bid you each a very Happy New Year. I hope that 2013 holds joy, prosperity, and the comfort of cheerful companions. If you have torn fabric of your own to restore, I hope for you, the chance to smooth the raveled edges of thread. At midnight on December 31st, take up a wooden spoon, go outside, and make some noise. Then drink a little hot chocolate, and nibble on some cookies   without regard to your vow to lose weight. And sleep. When you awaken, a whole year will be ahead of you, a  year with new chances to forge strong bonds, whole empty calendar pages to fill with delightful adventures, and open hours when you can settle down to browse the pages of the book you've been longing to read, or listen to the dreams of your children and the ambitions of your spouse.

A new year dawns. Make the best of it!

Mugwumpishly tendered,


Corinne Corley

Corinne Corley (left) and Genevieve Casey (right) at one of the quarterly art openings held at *Art @ Suite 100*, the public art space which Corley and her professional cohorts hosted from 2010 to 2017. Photograph seen behind them: *Floating* by Genevieve Casey

Corinne Corley — *(the child formerly known as 'Mary')* *hails from Jennings, Missouri, where she survived Catholic schools and learned everything she knows being the sixth child of eight. Her writing career began in 1970 with an essay for a Christian youth magazine in which she postulated God as a neuter gender being, for which the magazine paid $5.00. After a long, cherished, and sometimes amusing career as a Missouri attorney, she closed her law practice, sold her 100-year-old Brookside bungalow, and decamped to Northern California in a tiny house on wheels named "Angel's Haven". She has one child, three ex-husbands, and a solid tribe of friends without whom her life would be a wasteland of boredom and anxiety. You can find her most summers on a levee road in the California Delta hanging from her car door trying to capture the perfect photograph of a lone egret among the lofty piles of hyacinth floating down the San Joaquin River.*

Genevieve Casey — *has grown and lived in the Kansas City area, where she has focused on photography for the past 15 years. She uses ambient light and existing conditions to capture the beauty that exists in sometimes ordinary, and sometimes extraordinary settings. Her other hat is working in public health. Her photographic work is an outgrowth of her observation that finding ways to experience mindfulness and gratitude in our daily lives is essential for wellness. Genevieve's photography is about taking your time to slow down and notice the details, to observe the interesting and the beautiful everywhere. Nature is a constant inspiration for her work, though not the only source. Whether documenting nature, humans, or abandoned buildings, she prefers using ambient light and looking for different angles and perspectives to view her subjects.*